WILD DOG DREAMING

WILD DOG DREAMING

LOVE AND EXTINCTION

Deborah Bird Rose

UNIVERSITY OF VIRGINIA PRESS
CHARLOTTESVILLE AND LONDON

University of Virginia Press
© 2011 by the Rector and Visitors
of the University of Virginia
Printed in the United States of America
on acid-free paper

First published 2011

9 8 7 6 5 4 3 2 1

LIBRARY OF CONGRESS CATALOGING-IN-PUBLICATION DATA
Rose, Deborah Bird, 1946–
  Wild dog dreaming : love and extinction / Deborah Bird
Rose.
    p.   cm. — (Under the sign of nature: explorations in
ecocriticism)
  Includes bibliographical references and index.
  ISBN 978-0-8139-3091-6 (cloth : alk. paper) —
ISBN 978-0-8139-3107-4 (e-book)
  1. Dingo—Australia—Northern Territory—Anecdotes.
2. Dingo—Australia—Northern Territory—Effect of human
beings on. 3. Aboriginal Australians—Australia—Northern
Territory—Philosophy. 4. Dogs—Philosophy. 5. Endangered
species—Australia—Northern Territory. I. Title.
  QL795.D5R67 2011
  304.2'7—dc22

                              2010035062

Contents

Acknowledgments

So much gratitude! My father, David Rose, read an early version of this manuscript and offered perceptive and helpful advice throughout. Peter Boyle also read the whole manuscript with a thoughtful and probing intellect. Thom van Dooren read the whole thing, too, and was exceedingly helpful; his enthusiasm for the work carried me through some tough patches. In addition, the careful analytic readings of David Clark and Jim Hatley were absolutely crucial to bringing this book to full flower. Most of the Aboriginal teachers I rely on in this book are now dead. Writing is one of the ways I am able to continue to thank them by keeping their stories moving in the world. Old Tim, the clever man, had a hand in this book in ways that I will probably never fully understand.

Various chapters in this book were presented at seminars and conferences. I have benefited greatly from colleagues' questions, comments, feedback, and stimulation. Special thanks to the foundation members of the Ecological Humanities group with whom I workshopped many ideas: Natasha Fijn, Leah Gibbs, Bernadette Hince, George Main, Ingereth Macfarlane, Cameron Muir, Emily O'Gorman, Val Plumwood, Libby Robin, Thom van Dooren, Jessica Weir, thanks for all the great get-togethers. And thanks to the Bible and Critical Theory group, particularly Roland Boer, for keeping my engagements with the Bible relatively on track. Three special conferences were especially important in helping me develop my ideas: "Environments and Ecologies in an Expanded Field" (Adelaide, 2004), "'Be True to Earth': A Conference on Culture, Critical Theory and the Environment" (Melbourne, 2005), and "Emmanuel Levinas Centenary Conference: 'My Place in the Sun': Levinas Today" (Brisbane, 2006). Thanks to organizers and guiding spirits: Heather Kerr, Emily Potter, Kate Tucker, Kate Rigby, Michelle Boulos Walker, and Angela Hirst. Freya Mathews introduced me to the campfire method of dialogical exposition, and I am grateful for that and for the many sparks of inspiration we have shared.

A key member of our ecological humanities group was the late

Val Plumwood (see www.ecologicalhumanities.org). I am extremely grateful for all our conversations, and for her wonderfully critical and engaged mind and manner. She was never far from this manuscript both before and after her death; I miss her terribly.

I have carried this manuscript with me in my travels, and have found special delight in writing in different places. Thanks to friends and relations who gave me food, bed, and companionship while I wrote: Blunt Jackson, Freya Mathews, and others. Thanks, as well, to my favorite cafés: the Top Pot in Seattle, the Gods in Canberra, and Java Lava in Sydney.

Part of this book was written while I was a Senior Fellow in the Centre for Resource and Environmental Studies (now the Fenner School) at the Australian National University. It was completed in my position as Professor of Social Inclusion in the Centre for Research on Social Inclusion, Macquarie University. Special thanks to Banu Senay and Matt Chrulew for their assistance in finalizing the manuscript.

Versions of chapter 5, "Orion's Dog," have been published elsewhere: under the title "The Rivers of Babylon" in *Manoa* 18, no. 2 (Winter 2006): 1–6; under the title "Journeys: Distance, Proximity and Death" in *Landscapes of Exile,* ed. Anna Haebish and Baden Offord (London: Peter Lang, 2008); and under the title "Rivers of Babylon" in *Stories of Belonging,* ed. Kali Wendorf (Werriewood, New South Wales: Finch, 2009). An earlier version of chapter 8, "What If the Angel of History Were a Dog?" was published in *Cultural Studies Review* 12, no. 1 (2006): 67–78.

The story of the dog massacre is an extract from a short story written by Ronald and Catherine Berndt about life on northern cattle stations, sent to Linden A. Mander, Professor of Political Science, University of Washington, Seattle. It is quoted in Geoffrey Gray, *Abrogating Responsibility: Vesteys, Anthropology and the Future of Aboriginal People* (Melbourne: Australian Scholarly Publishing, 2010), and reproduced with the kind permission of Ronald and Catherine Berndt's literary executor, John E. Stanton.

I am grateful to Stephen Edgar for permission to reprint his poem "Chernobyl Dogs," first published in *Where the Trees Were,* (Charnwood, Australian Capital Territory: Ginninderra Press, 1999). Finally, I thank Peter Boyle and MTC Cronin for permission to pub-

ix

.australianhumanitiesreview.org/). Boyle's "Travelling in a Caravan"
and Cronin's "Whatever Becomes Itself" were first published in
AHR, no. 39–40 (2006), special section: "Ecopoetics and the Ecological Humanities in Australia."

WILD DOG DREAMING

1. Where Shall Wisdom Be Found?

A few years ago my friend Jessica stopped by the office to tell me something awful. Not far from Canberra she had seen a tree that was strung up with dead dingoes. Horrified and inexorably curious, I went to see for myself. It was as she had told me: the dingoes were suspended by their hind legs, heads down, bodies extended, another "strange fruit" in the annals of cruelty. I prowled the edges of the area, my mouth dry and my throat constricting as the smell of decay and the horror reached into me. Vertigo was causing a sense of estrangement, and I could not be sure where I was, so that I kept looking back to the truck to remind myself that this was the twenty-first century, that I'd driven here from my home in the national capital of Australia, that I was on an ordinary dirt road near the edge of a national park, that in a few minutes I would get back in the truck and drive away. In some fundamental sense I was lost. *Dear God*, I thought, *where are you?*

Stories flashed across my mind. Many of my Aboriginal teachers had told me long and wonderful accounts of dingoes. "Dog's a big boss," Old Tim Yilngayarri, the clever man, had said. "You've gotta leave him. No more killing." He was speaking within a context in which dingoes are regularly poisoned and shot, and he knew, as did I, that the shadow of death falls heavily upon their future. They are not the first animal to be facing extinction, and they will not be the last. But they are one of the few whose extinction is actively being sought by some segments of human society. The Regulatory Review Committee of the parliament of the state of New South Wales (NSW) put the case succinctly, albeit bureaucratically: "It is however anomalous that the main NSW initiative to conserve existing Dingo populations is being undertaken under an Act that will classify them, statewide, as a pest requiring eradication."[1]

This "anomaly" is best encountered in the wider context of human-driven disaster. According to Paul Crutzen, the Nobel laureate who coined the term "Anthropocene," the influence of humanity on Earth in recent centuries is so significant as to constitute a new geological era. Global climate change is altering how we understand the Earth system, and we are in the midst of the sixth great extinction event on Earth, the first to be caused by a single species, namely our own. Anthropogenic extinction, as it is called in conservation biology, is a fact of death that is growing exponentially. We are entering an era of loss of life unprecedented in human history. Indeed, as E. O. Wilson describes it, we are plummeting into an "Age of Loneliness."[2]

The question, of course, is: if we humans are the cause, can we change ourselves enough to change our impacts? This question is brought vividly to our attention by the anthropologist Kay Milton. She notes the need for urgent action, and she notes that many calls to action have fear as an underlying motivating force. Milton draws on research that shows clearly that fear often is an extremely unsatisfactory driver, eliciting denial as much as action.[3] In this work I take up an alternative driving emotion. "People save what they love," says Michael Soulé, the great conservation biologist. He expresses an almost despairing concern over the current biodiversity extinction crisis, and he asks one of the most important questions of our time: Are humans capable of loving, and therefore of caring for, the animals and plants that are currently losing their lives in a growing cascade of extinctions? The power of love is awesome, as everyone who has loved will know. But equally, love is complex and full of problems as well as possibilities. William Stegner said it best in relation to place, and his words are applicable across all other ecological domains of our lives: "I really only want to say that we can love a place and still be dangerous to it."[4]

Love in the time of extinctions, therefore, calls forth another set of questions. Who are we, as a species? How do we fit into the Earth system? What ethics call to us? How to find our way into new stories to guide us, now that so much is changing? How to invigorate love and action in ways that are generous, knowledgeable, and life-affirming?

I have developed the idea of *ecological existentialism* to address the questions about who we are and how we fit. Ecological existentialism pulls together two major shifts in worldview: the end of certainty and the end of atomism. From certainty the shift is to uncertainty. From atomism the shift is to connectivity. The West has reached these big shifts through the working of its own intellectual and social history. From our current position it becomes possible to open new conversations with people whose histories are completely different, but whose worldviews work with uncertainty and connectivity. This is a moment for new conversations and new synergies.

The question of finding our way into new ways of understanding and acting is addressed through dialogue. Stories encounter each other and become entangled. They stick in unexpected places and spark up new thoughts. Many of the stories I recount arise out of my experiences with Aboriginal people in North Australia. More than a quarter of a century ago I left my home country, the United States, in order to live for a number of years with Aboriginal people in the communities of Yarralin and Lingara. I learned all that I could—all that people wanted to teach me and all that I was capable of absorbing—of their philosophical ecology.[5] The colonizing history of this great tropical savannah country is tough. White settlers established broadacre cattle properties across this savannah region about 120 years ago, and after an initial period of overt and often extreme violence, most of the Aboriginal survivors settled into life on cattle properties where they worked as an unpaid and unfree labor force for many decades. Since the 1970s, the most oppressive aspects of colonization have been shifted, but in spite of decolonizing legislation, many colonial relations of power are alive and well.[6]

I lived with people, sharing events and conversations, hunting, cooking, eating, traveling, mourning, rejoicing, laughing, singing, dancing, taking care of children. My teachers and I have asked each other questions, probed each other's values and worldviews, worked together on land claims, and sought by many means to understand each other. We've gone fishing, hunted and collected food together, eaten together and exchanged food with each other, buried the dead, wept, and welcomed new people into the world. I have come to understand that my teachers experience kinship with plants and animals at close quarters. Their relationships are tactile, and are embedded in creation, ethics, and accountability. And so it is that life within a system of cross-species kinship is in dreadful peril at this time. The animals and plants that are dying out are not so much vulnerable, endangered, or extinct species, but more significantly are vulnerable and dying members of the family. People's experience of extinction is up-close and very personal.

The people who have taught me have faced extinction themselves. They've lived through massacres, near slavery, and many other forms of cruelty, and still they tell their stories, and still they are generous in their teachings. There is an intensity within people's generosity that arises from their sense of having deep and serious understandings that other people should be listening to. As my teacher Daly Pulkara said, "We have listened to your stories. You, you Whitefella, you can listen to stories too." He was referring to his own stories, of course, and he had a reason: "I tell you: nothing can forget about that Law." He wanted people to listen because he knew himself to be giving an account of how the world really is. Aboriginal people's accounts of how the world is and how they as humans fit into it speak to both the local and the universal. Their stories are always grounded in specific places and creatures. At the same time, many of my teachers, like Aboriginal people around the world, are certain that their stories also express accounts of how life on Earth really is—for everyone. A good example is cross-species kinship. All my teachers were born into kinship with various animals, plants, and countries. The relationships were specific, and had limits—to be related to some meant not being related to others. The question that arises, for them and for me, is: Is such a kinship a foundational condition of human life? Science today answers this question in the affirmative. Many Aboriginal people also affirm universality. The Aboriginal actor, dancer, and philosopher David Gulpilil stated the case in his own poetic prose: "We are brothers and sisters of the world. Doesn't matter if you're bird, snake, fish, kangaroo: One Red Blood."[7]

In bringing some powerful Indigenous stories into conversation around the tormented questions of life and death, love and extinction, I also draw on some of the great stories of my own Western tradition. Stephen Kepnes's definition of narrative biblical theology guides the process of bringing stories into encounter. "Narrative Biblical theology," he writes, "involves a retelling of the narratives of the Bible in such a way that the central issues of the contemporary situation are expressed and addressed."[8] I am stretching the method beyond biblical narratives, and some of my encounters are partial because the intention is to stretch only one particular question. Equally, although it may not be accurate to suggest that working with Old Tim Yilngayarri's stories of dingoes and death is a way of doing narrative theology, the spirit of the endeavor remains the same. Narratival encounters aim for truth; and truth, in my context of writing, is the spark that illuminates the ethical proximity of others—all others, all living beings, all who are, in the great term of the philosopher Val Plumwood, "our Earth others."

When I stood before the defenseless bodies of dead dingoes, I was face-to-face with an event that encapsulates major questions of humanity and our ethical relationships with Earth life. I have written this book to explore a number of those questions from a range of perspectives. I draw on the teachings of wise people, some of whom are living, and many of whom are dead. I draw on some ancient stories as well as many that are contemporary, and I draw on teachers whose life experiences and cultures differ in the extreme. The conversation is open, and my words aim to draw readers into heightened awareness of their own possibilities for ethical encounter and action. At every step I am influenced by the philosopher Emil Fackenheim.[9] He wrote in the aftermath of the Nazi Holocaust, and he was seeking ways to "mend the world" without pretending that world-shattering events can ever be wholly undone or overcome. I believe that the current extinction crisis is an Earth-shattering disaster, one that cannot be unmade, and in that sense cannot be mended, but yet one toward which we owe an ethical response that includes turning toward others in the hopes of mending at least some of the damage. "Turning toward" (*Tikkun*) in Fackenheim's philosophy, is an ethics of motion toward encounter, a willingness to situate one's self so as to be available to the call of others. It is a willingness toward dialogue, a willingness toward responsibility, a choice for encounter and response, a turning toward rather than a turning away.

Wild Wisdom

Lev Shestov the philosopher and Old Tim Yilngayarri the Australian Aboriginal "clever man" were two of my great teachers in life. They shared a fabulous glee in their awareness that the living world

is more complicated, less predictable, more filled with transformations, uncertainty, and fantastic eruptions of life's mysteries than is
allowed of in ordinary thought. Each in his own way was a holy fool,
and each brought a wild wisdom into the world.

I fell in love with Lev Shestov when I discovered his stunning
essays that rail against rationalist-dominated modernity and offer a
"crazy" vision of a world in which life exceeds knowledge, and in
which mutability and uncertainty are blessed emanations of life.
Against the prevailing ethos of secular modernity, Shestov writes in
passionate exuberance to create a philosophical celebration of the
joyous mysteries of the unpredictabilities of life on Earth.

Shestov's deep plea for the Western world is that we regain the
capacity to acknowledge that the Earth is good. In a particularly
powerful passage, he asks, "Why should creation not be perfect? . . .
No one, neither of our time nor even of the Middle Ages, dared to
admit that the biblical 'very good' corresponded to reality, that the
world created by God" was truly good.[10] His desire, the desire within
the whole of the work, as I understand it, is to restore to European
humanity the capacity to see the world in its goodness—to find contemporary ways to recover the "divine 'very good'."[11]

Old Tim was one of my most generous teachers. He was born
about 1905 in his mother's country, the clan territory known as
Layit. The country is demarcated by a creek that is a tributary of the
Wickham River, itself a tributary of the Victoria River, which is one
of the great monsoonal rivers of North Australia. The region had
only recently been occupied by White settlers when Tim was born,
and the frontier pastoralists were still struggling to protect their
cattle against the difficulties of weather, terrain, cattle thieves, Aboriginal people, and nonhuman predators such as crocodiles. For a
decade or so, the warfare was intense as Aboriginal people sought to
defend their home countries. Pastoralists were aided by a mounted
constable, and the record books show that he made numerous pa-
trols into Layit in search of "cattle killers" (Aborigines).[12]

By the time Tim was born, the worst of the warfare was over. His
parents had joined the Whitefellas on Victoria River Downs Station,
and he lived most of his adult life in the outback pastoral society
of White overlords and Indigenous workers. He was fluent in Aboriginal Pastoral English and for many decades had been a cowboy.

At the same time, he was fluent in several Indigenous languages. He had been through all the initiation ceremonies for men, and had become a Lawman himself, an expert and leader in knowledge and ritual. In addition, he was a clever man, a man with extraordinary powers. In fact, he was the only person I've been lucky enough to meet who could describe having been taken to the Sky country, which is where his powers were bestowed on him. By the time I met him, Old Tim had lost much of his power, and no one in that area has demonstrated similar gifts. It may be, as some suggest, that such power is being lost in that part of the world, but perhaps not. Life is full of surprises.

When I met Old Tim in 1980, he was already old: grey-haired, and sporting a wonderful long white beard. His humor was un-dimmed, and his passionate attachment to dogs was legendary. One of Old Tim's names was Old Bogaga, Bogaga being his father's country. It was an area away to the southwest of us, and was full of important Dingo sites and songs. The old man had a special re-lationship with the wild dogs of Australia known as dingoes, and he told long, fabulous stories about shared kinship: about how dogs and humans have a common origin and destiny. Unlike many In-digenous creation stories, which tell of specific places and specific people, Old Tim's dingo stories are meant to concern all human be-ings. These are stories of death and what happens after, of the desire to dominate, of the failure to reciprocate, and of the deeply abid-ing connections between humans and nonhumans, expressed most forcibly as kinship. In Tim's stories, dingoes are the ancestors of *all* human beings; they give us our faces, our stance, our death, and the return that cycles us through the bodies of other living creatures. At first there was only one creature—a dog-human person—and this creature differentiated himself/herself, inaugurating both dog-per-sons and human-persons. Dogs/dingoes and humans are still close kin because of their shared origins. Old Tim universalized this story, ensuring that we understand that the story is for all of us: "Dream-ing [creators] worked that way for everyone, White lady, Aboriginal men, all the same. They walk, they stand up, they're finished being dogs now, they're proper humans, women and men. Mother and Fa-ther Dingo made Aboriginal people. White children come out of a white dog." Think about it: to look at the face of a dog is to see your own ancestor and your contemporary kin. It is to see mothers and fathers, sisters and brothers. They still walk with us and nuzzle us with their long-nosed faces. Without them we would not be who we are, and their faces turn toward us in the knowledge that we are here together, all of us, living and dying in our related ways.

Rain Dogs

Tom Waits has an album called *Rain Dogs* on which he sings the lives of the lost, the homeless, those without direction. Dogs find their way in the world primarily by scent. "Rain dogs" are the ones who are lost because the rain has washed away all their familiar markers.[13] No longer knowing how to find their way home, they stray in vain, trotting here, sniffing there, searching for the way back. Dogs are conscious of their companions, being social animals as well as being co-evolved with humans, and so there is a doubled sorrow when they lose the scents. They've lost their way home, and they've lost their companions. Waits is singing about human beings, of course, and he includes himself in the story: "for I am a rain dog too."

There are two major moments in the history of the West when humans have lost their bearings and have felt themselves to be homeless. The first occurred about two thousand years ago, and the second began with modernity and reached its peak in the twentieth century. The sociologist Hans Jonas puts forward the idea that in both eras there was a change in people's "vision of nature" (or "cosmic environment"), and that this change gave rise both to ancient Gnosticism and to contemporary nihilism.[14] Jonas's theory, then, is that as our understanding of our relationships with nature changes, so our philosophical ecology changes. Our understanding of ourselves as a certain kind of creature with certain meanings and purposes in relation to the living world, in Jonas's view, is wrapped up in our vision of humanity and nature.

Jonas identifies the centuries 100 BC–AD 400 as the crucial period "in which the spiritual destiny of the Western world took shape."[15] Then, as in the modern era, there was a shift in people's understanding of nature, or what we might call the way of the living world. This change involved a loss of the sense of connection, and it led to a terrible loneliness. That feeling of alienation, of not being at home on Earth, engendered a wider mood of forlornness and dread.[16] In the crucial centuries just preceding and following the life of Jesus, the classical world was falling apart politically and morally, and the worldview that had pervaded it seemed no longer adequate. To many people, God appeared to be distant, the world seemed evil, and people wrote of a sense of being thrown into a place that was not home.[17]

In analyzing the modern era, philosophers look to Descartes for an extreme expression of a dualism that totally separates humanity from nature. In Descartes' view, nature is nothing but matter. Only humans think, and human thought is not part of nature but rather is that which separates humans from nature. There is then a thorough separation—a thinking reality confined to humans, and the mindless matter that makes up the rest of the living world. In their superiority to nature, humans are foreigners on Earth. Part of the peril of this position is in the mechanistic role of God as the first cause. God got everything moving and then stepped back, leaving the world ticking along according to immutable laws, and leaving man alone in a world that fundamentally did not concern Him. Lonely as this was, Western thought went on to consider the absence, and even the death, of God. Once that vision of God was lost, when God became dead, nature too became effectively dead, for God was all that had ever animated it.[18]

Heidegger famously took this separation as far as possible in his search for the nature of being. He proposed that humanity is uniquely alive, uniquely aware of its own being, and thus unique in the cosmos. He writes, "The being that exists is man. Man alone exists. Rocks are, but they do not exist. Trees are, but they do not exist. Angels are, but they do not exist. God is, but he does not exist." Heidegger is not claiming that everything other than man is unreal, but rather that only man looks to his existence and asks why it is so.[19]

Martin Buber's description of the process of increasing human solitude is eloquent: "In the history of the human spirit man again and again becomes solitary, that is, he finds himself alone with a universe which has become alien and uncanny. . . . There is a way leading from one age of solitude to the next, that is, that each solitude is colder and stricter than the preceding, and salvation from it ever more difficult." He goes on to describe a moment when it was no longer possible to reach out to the divine, a moment announced by Nietzsche under the banner "God is dead." This was the state of philosophical thought which announced and inaugurated contemporary European nihilism.[20]

The Anthropocene is bringing us into a new era of solitude, one marked less by our fragmented vision of ourselves than by the actual loss of co-evolved life. As Earth others depart, never to return, we face a diminishing and impoverished world, and equally, we face new, agonizingly lonely, questions about the meaning of our existence.

The separation and loneliness of modernity go hand in hand with the astonishing technological brilliance of our time. All of us who have benefited from the wonders of the twentieth century—antibiotics, computers, world travel, for example—will be grateful to have lived in such an era. At the same time, we increasingly come to understand, as Jonas reminds us so succinctly, "the danger of disaster attending the . . . ideal of power over nature through scientific technology arises not so much from any shortcomings of its performance as from the magnitude of success."[21] In worshipping the god of progress, we have unleashed the dogs of war, and it seems that the war dogs are us.

We live within this most recent rain-dog moment, and our challenge is to find scents and guides to help us find our way back home. Our imperative is to recover or discover connectivity and the radical awareness of being at home that emerges as we embed ourselves ever more complexly into the life of the world. The world is suffering, life is dying, and the project of embedding ourselves exposes us consciously to peril. To understand this is to become radically conscious of our own frailty. At the same time, let us remember that rain dogs are beautiful in their valor as well as in their vulnerability. Consciousness of connectedness entails choices made with courage and directed toward care.

The philosopher Erazim Kohak tells us, "Perhaps the most basic ecological experience is that of an audacious generosity, of daring to love all the suffering, perishing creation."[22] My stories follow in Kohak's footsteps, and are guided by his assertion that "in the world of our lives . . . there is a truth, the basic truth of the goodness of life, of the badness of its negation and of the evil of the will to negate."[23] To think from a kinship standpoint about our relationships with animals in this time of extinctions is to open up radically challenging questions. What is our role in this world? If others matter, as they seem to, what about us? Do *we* matter, and if so, why? What should *we* be doing? These are questions that bring us to ethics. Throughout this book I am working with Newton's elegant and inspired definition of ethics as "recursive, contingent, and interactive dramas of encounter and recognition."[24]

The chapters that follow make use of a few terms of art that, like ethics, I shall define in advance. These are not dictionary definitions, but rather working definitions that help me say what I mean to say as I write about difficult and challenging questions.

DREAMING: Australian Aboriginal modification of English to denote the creators, the origins, the process of creation, the continuities of coming into being and coming into pattern (see chapter 2).

BECOMING: The conditions of life are not set once and for all; living and nonliving beings are works in progress.

BECOMING WITH: Living and nonliving beings are mutually interdependent; our lives are lived in connection; each becoming depends on our relationships with other living and nonliving beings.

BECOMING HUMAN: Humanity is an interspecies collaborative project; we become who we are in the company of other beings; we are not alone. (With thanks to Anna Tsing, Paul Shepard, and the Aboriginal philosopher Mary Graham.)[25]

CONNECTIVITY: (1) In ecological science, connectivity refers to exchange pathways (for energy, information, living things); the greater the number and complexity of pathways, the greater the biodiversity; (2) more widely, exchange pathways may include stories, songs, forms of address; (3) at the foundation—the bonds that sustain the life system of Earth.

COMMUNITY OF FATE: As living beings come into life collaboratively and mutually, their fates are intermeshed; we live and die together, and no one, ultimately, is isolated from calamity. (With thanks to Robyn Eckersley and Thom van Dooren.)[26]

WORLD MAKING: (1) In becoming with others we bring forth worlds of action and meaning, with varied possibilities for life and for death; (2) the fact that living and nonliving beings are works in progress, are always in states of becoming (or un-becoming), means that the Earth itself is a work-in-progress. We are, all of us living beings, engaged in world making (and unmaking). In considering world making, our guiding questions must be: Is mutuality sustained? Are self and others flourishing? Are the possibilities for life enhanced? (With thanks to Hannah Arendt and Donna Haraway.)[27]

ETHICS: Interactive dramas of encounter and recognition. To come face-to-face with others, to recognize and respond to the other's call; to grasp the fact that we are mutually becoming with each other. (With thanks to Levinas and Newton.)[28]

OPENING/OPENING UP: Becoming involved in intense dramas of encounter and recognition; where world making happens; transformative processes; the process of ethics—being touched and responding. (With apologies to Heidegger, Haraway, and others.)

GOD: One way of talking about power, and its absence.

DEATH WORLD/DEATH SPACE: Where worlds and lives are unmade; in the context of the Holocaust, where genocide is practiced and both time and becoming are extinguished (with thanks to Hatley).[29] In the context of extinctions, where the 4-billion-year history of life on Earth is being terminated.

DUALISMS AND HYPERSEPARATION: Dualisms are the product of an either/or way of thinking that sets up opposites and defines them in relation to each other with one pole superior, the other pole inferior; hyperseparation is the stretching of dualisms so that the two poles have nothing in common: in this book, the mind/matter, or culture/nature dualism is a key focus. (With thanks to Val Plumwood.)

WILD: I use the term in a specifically Western sense—the wild is a refusal to submit to the conventional limitations of Western thought, including refusal to submit to illusions of certainty, to dualisms and to human-centrism, among other limitations. (With both thanks and apologies to David Abram.)[30]

TURNING TOWARD: An ethical practice that acknowledges histories of distance and disaster, and yet still seeks to be responsive to others' suffering and joy, and to others' life and death. Always situated in history and in relationship, turning toward seeks to mend relationships, to make worlds that are hospitable to life. (With thanks to Emil Fackenheim.)[31]

FACE-TO-FACE: The term of ethical encounter inspired by the work of philosopher Emmanuel Levinas, who writes that in the face of the other I am always responsible. To ask to whom, or to what, does one come face-to-face is to ask to whom or to what am I responsible? This is the question of our time.

REALITY, THE REAL: Vicki Hearne's passionate statement of connectivity can be read as a manifesto for the real: "To be fully human is to recognize everyone and everything in the universe as both Other and Beloved, and that . . . entails granting that the world is authentic and meaningful without demanding proof."[32]

Firestick Wisdom

My great fortune was to work on numerous Aboriginal claims to land in many parts of the Northern Territory from central deserts to monsoon savannas to coastal floodplains, sandy peninsulas, and offshore islands. One area where I spent a glorious amount of time was the Simpson Desert of Central Australia. The Simpson is one of the world's great sand ridge deserts. Summer temperatures can exceed 120°F (50°C), and much of the region receives an annual rainfall of less than 5 inches (13 cm) in an "average" year, although averages don't mean much in this environment.

We traveled in convoy—Aboriginal traditional owners, land council staff, and the Aboriginal land commissioner and his party, of which I was a member. We were packed into four-wheel-drive vehicles, and we traveled along rough little tracks that wound their way through or cut across all these dunes. We visited sacred sites throughout the desert, and those of us who were outsiders came to understand how a desert that seems so inhospitable to life is actually Aboriginal country—the home to all the living beings whose travels fan out across the desert with the rain, and who converge on tiny waterholes when the episodic rains depart. We learned that the desert is crisscrossed with Dreaming tracks, and that people's lives are part of these tracks because people are born into the stories and places of Dreaming sites and songlines.

One of the leading figures in a number of these claims was Edward Johnson, a man of extraordinary knowledge and tough sensibility. He was blessed with a delightful sense of humor, and he spoke quirky and expressive English. He was a small man with a personality that outshone people twice his size. His age and his way with words, his humor and his directness, made him a superb witness, as did his commanding presence. He stood at sacred sites and spoke of the stories and songs, the rituals, and the connectivities between different Dreaming tracks; and he spoke of the people, the animals, the plants, and the water. He riveted our attention.

Mr. Johnson told of how each different group of people is responsible for the knowledge of its country and for the Dreaming Law of the place, and how the countries and groups connect up through the songlines. He took us to "handover" places, where one group hands the song on to the next group. On one occasion when he was asked to explain these responsibilities in greater detail, he responded by talking about what makes a good neighbor in this desert region. His words are emblazoned in my mind: "A good neighbour tells on and on, you know, that same rolling."[33] I can feel the stories rolling across the desert, carrying the local into connectivity and into wider contexts. I hear Mr. Johnson articulating an ethics of story—an ethics of coming face-to-face with neighbors and their stories, and responding by keeping them moving. In the spirit of neighborliness, I am endeavoring to sustain "that same rolling," to keep some of the stories, or the spirit of the stories, moving along in the contexts of my lifeworld.

But ways of keeping stories rolling constitute yet another interesting question. Here, too, I learned a lot from Old Tim. We talked together on many occasions over the years, and from time to time he would add another dimension to the repertoire of Dingo stories. They form a loose body of stories that tell about life's becoming, and about becoming human. He offered his wisdom in his own (Aboriginal) fashion: in performance, and in bits and pieces of conversation that challenge the listener to make the connections. It was not meant to be a closed system. Old Tim kept it open to the world by refraining from formalizing it. I honor and respect his method, and therefore do not want to slip into trying to make it something other than he intended. Throughout this book I return to Old Tim and his stories with the intention of keeping the wisdom rolling, allowing it to accumulate, and refraining from declaring final meanings.

Let them come together, then, the stories that take us into Shestov's wild exuberance, Old Tim's kinship with animals, and the complexities of Soulé's question about love. Imagine a campfire where the flames are not too high, the coals are glowing brightly, and people are chatting and telling stories, letting the flow of ideas take them into new places. This kind of conversation—open, interested, and eventful—sparks up ideas and insights. Around the fire are Old Tim and other senior Aboriginal people. Some of the stories they tell will be hard to understand. They speak of the goodness of life, but they are not always packaged in convenient forms. There are some philosophers here, too—Lev Shestov, Erazim Kohak, and the great feminist scholars Donna Haraway, Freya Mathews, and Val Plumwood. A few theologians, biologists, and ecologists will drop in, and the existential theologian Martin Buber is present throughout. There will be some poets, singer-songwriters, essayists, and storytellers. I expect a family of dingoes will join us from time to time.

A special guest at this fire is the late Emmanuel Levinas. He was quite clearly the greatest philosopher of ethics of the twentieth century. In the words of Michael Oppenheim, Levinas was not only a philosopher, but a thinker who sought to undo Western philosophy "by way of a passionate ethical protest."[34] Levinas writes persuasively for the idea that one comes into being only through relationships, and that therefore one is always indebted to the others who precede us; one is always in ethical relationships that call for response. He offers the beautiful images of the face and the call as the foundations of ethical response. The call of the other, the face of the other, the responsibilities to and for the other form the foundation of this beautiful relational philosophy. The one big limit in Levinas's thought is that he confined his ethics to humans. He is a special guest in the conversation around the fire because we all want to know how his philosophy may be challenged, and whether it will survive, when the call of the other is a bark or a howl, and the face of the other is an animal.

And what of my own position? My love of the living world has been with me "forever"; it was radically enhanced, and my understandings were immensely deepened through my life with Aboriginal people in Australia. Given that religious thought runs through this book, it seems appropriate to say that I was raised in a religious family. As a child I found organized religion both fascinating and appalling, and nothing in adult life has pulled me far from that view. At the same time, I experience the love that draws me (like many others) into these deep stories. I hope never to be far from the cadences of the poetry, and I am grateful that some key religious values such as concern for justice and respect for the integrity of others pervade my life. In seeking meeting points between what I value in religion and what I love in the world, I keep thinking of the old joke: What do you call an agnostic insomniac who suffers from dyslexia? I did not choose this, but perhaps I am the person who stays awake at night wondering if there really is a Dog.

2. Looking into Extinction

When Theresa's mother was so sick that everyone feared she was dying, she was surrounded by the family. We cried over her and sang to her, and massaged her arms and legs to keep her circulation going. The clever man, Old Tim, went on a journey following her spirit as it was leaving her body. He was calling it to come back. There came a moment when he realized that this spirit could not come back, that this woman was entering the death place, and that now the family would have to stop trying to hold her back and try to help her through. Thanks to Old Tim, we all knew that this was death. Theresa's mother died a few hours later.

The wet season had begun, and we were flooded in at the time. We had no radio communication and no other access to society beyond the community, so we buried her quickly without interference from secular or religious authorities. The family organized everything; they sang the mourning songs, swept the community with green leaves to wipe out all her tracks, and smoked the house she died in and the people who had been with her. Her name became taboo as the absence caused by her death was transformed into a living memory. The funeral sent the old woman back to her country, tying her death into the ongoing life of her place on Earth.

The Aboriginal concept of "country" is central to understanding how death is turned back toward life. Country is a spatial unit—large enough to support a group of people, small enough to be intimately known in every detail, and home to the living things whose lives come and go in that place. The origins of country are in creation. The Australian continent is crisscrossed with the tracks of the creator beings, called Dreamings in Aboriginal English. Walking, slithering, crawling, flying, swimming, chasing, hunting, weeping, dying, giving birth, Dreamings were performing rituals, distributing plants and marking the zones of animal and plant distributions, making the landforms and water, and making the relationships between one place and another, one species and another. They were leaving parts or essences of themselves; they would look back in sorrow, and then continue traveling, changing languages, changing songs, changing identity. They shifted their shape from animal to human and back to animal again, and as they acted they were becoming ancestral to life on Earth. Multispecies kin groups are the result of creation, and the term "Dreaming" applies to the ancestors of these groups.

The kangaroo people and the kangaroo animals, for example, have become a family (clan), and the dingo people and dingoes are the same, as are many others. Family members take care of each other, watch out for each other's interests, defend each other against outsiders, and generally seek to sustain both their connections with other families and the internal integrity of their own family. Within these country-based multispecies families, there is a moral proposition that is not so much a rule as a statement of how life works: a country and its living beings take care of their own. Care of country is a matter of both self-interest and interest for others. An understanding of connectivity promotes long-term purposefulness in life and long-term commitments to country's varied life in all its life-and-death diversity.

This Dreaming or totemic way of being in the world is a form of animism, defined in a new and excellent study by Graham Harvey as the recognition "that the world is full of persons, only some of whom are human, and that life is always lived in relationship with others."[1] Ethics of love and care within this context do not exclude animals, and they do not exclude death. In a world of hunting and gathering, death and continuity are core aspects of the integrity of life, and are always unavoidably present in people's lives and minds. An ethical response to the call of others does not hinge on killing or not killing. It hinges on taking responsibility for one's actions. Responsibilities are complexly situated in time and place; most of all they are up-close; face-to-face in both life and death.

When the family sang Theresa's mother home to country, they were returning her to the place from which she had come. They expected that she would remain at home there, keeping the country healthy and nourishing. The connectivities between the person, her country, and her Dreaming were visible after the old woman's death. Her main Dreaming was Lightning, and for several nights following her death the sky to the south of us, where her country was, absolutely jumped with life. There were forks and spirals, bursts and trails; Lightning put out an extravagant show, leaping, rolling, and chasing itself across the southern sky.

Well, people die; there's nothing novel in that. But something more than death had stalked these Aboriginal people for decades under the name of colonization and in the form of massacres, starvation, influenza, syphilis, leprosy, and much more.[2] Old Tim and his people had faced the possibility of their own extinction. They'd seen clans die out, and they'd grouped countries together so that there would be someone living who would be able to take care when the last remaining clanspeople were gone. Old Tim was one such survivor. He and other powerful and intelligent people did their utmost to learn, to hold, and to teach so that the lives of their forebears, both immediate and extended, would not disappear without a trace.

My understanding of death matured during my years with Aboriginal people. Death makes claims upon all of us, I learned, claims that invoke our ethics, our love, our compassion, our sorrow, and

Old Tim Yilngayarri and some of his dogs, in the cattle yard at Yarralin, 1981.
(PHOTO COURTESY OF DARRELL LEWIS)

our future. Every death is a complex event, and we who are alive are privileged to be able to look into death and see the love and loss, the rupture and connection. On all of us death makes this claim: that we look into the eyes of the dying and not flinch, that we reach out to hold and to help. Further, that we respond to death by affirming the continuity of life across the generations. And further yet, that we affirm and sustain multispecies connections.

For some 4 billion years, life and death have been working together, each finding its own level in relation to the other, and together sustaining a family of life on Earth, a family that is always changing, always finding connections, generating fit, seeking an always shifting balance in an Earth system that is itself far from equilibrium.[3] Lynn Margulis and Dorion Sagan write in their wonderful book *What Is Life?* that life is "matter gone wild, capable of choosing its own direction in order to indefinitely forestall the inevitable moment of thermodynamic equilibrium—death."[4] We humans emerged in dynamic relationships with animals and plants; with them we share our dependence on water and air, and we share basic energy and basic substance: blood, and its plant counterpart, chlorophyll, in particular. Understanding how we fit into the community of life and death is not really an optional extra. As Thom van Dooren puts it: we are "interwoven into a system in which we live and die *with* others, live and die *for* others."[5]

The struggle to sustain connections across death is analyzed admirably by the American scholar James Hatley. He works with the "death narrative" concept in his study of suffering and genocide.[6] A death narrative in human terms situates death and the dead within a historical community. Hatley writes, "What is important about a death narrative is that one's own passing away becomes a gift for those who follow, as well as an address to them. Death narratives are vocative; they call to one's survivors for some mode of response."[7] The death narrative "is a transitive crossing-over that generates a new existence characterized in terms of a new responsibility."[8]

As I have encountered Aboriginal people and their understandings of death, I have been moved to bring the death narrative concept into ecological domains.[9] Country itself is a narrative of all the living things, the humans and all the others whose lives contributed to the life of the country. From the perspective of country, a death narrative binds the living and the dead into an ecological community (not just a historical community), working with multispecies crossovers as well as generational crossovers. When death is embedded within a system of multispecies kinship, animals that die are members of families; they have human kin as well as kin of their own species. In these Aboriginal families there are many deaths, not only because this is how life always ends, but because these people are hunters. Their own lives depend on the food that is the bodies of other animals, and every hunted animal is someone's family. Death is extremely intimate, and all deaths matter.

In contrast, our Western tradition has long dedicated itself to finding ways to turn our eyes away from the deaths of animals, and in fact some philosophers contend that that turning away is absolutely central to our understanding of who we are.[10] The main method has been to imagine a hyperseparated dualism, or incommensurable and oppositional difference, between humans and other animals. Humans are the creatures with minds, or culture; animals are "mere" nature.[11] Toward the end of his life, the French philosopher Jacques Derrida began writing about animals and humans, querying the philosophical nature of the boundary between them. He writes that rather than an absolute boundary, there is a multiple and heterogeneous border zone.[12] In this he parallels the more deeply engaged work of ecological philosophers such as Val Plumwood, Freya Mathews, and Donna Haraway. Along with these philosophers, I query the idea of a border between humans and other animals, however porous, focusing rather on fields or patterns of differentiation and connection. Compassion, mateship, mutual trust, and all manner of relationships are articulated across patterns of connection and differentiation, including hunting, eating, dying, and being eaten.

The significance of Derrida's work for my context here is that he connects animal deaths with genocide, and that he connects factory farming with extinctions. He does not develop these connections, but in making the juxtapositions he points to a convergence of important issues.[13] When Derrida writes of the current relationships between humans and animals he means, in fact, a certain set of postindustrial humans. This is not a universal proposition, but it is a significant one: "No one can deny seriously, or for very long, that men do all they can in order to dissimulate this cruelty [to animals] or to hide it from themselves, in order to organize on a global scale the forgetting or misunderstanding of this violence that some would compare to the worst cases of genocide (there are also animal genocides: the number of species endangered because of man takes one breath away)."[14] Derrida's chief concern is with the industrialized production of corpses for meat, and of course he is not the first to bring the term "genocide" into the discourse of mass-produced animal deaths (see chapters 3 and 8).

In juxtaposing the deaths of humans and other animals, the purpose is to examine ways that the boundary of difference is policed so that it becomes possible to ignore animal deaths. One form of policing works with the idea that animal deaths are of less ethical considerability, to use the philosophers' term, than are human deaths. The idea here is that one important difference between animals and humans is that animals are those who can be killed with impunity.[15] Many philosophers look to Heidegger for an intensely strong statement of this boundary. In his view, animals are not fully alive the way humans are, and their deaths are not deaths as human deaths are. Animals simply cease to exist, he said. It is humans who die significantly; an animal's life is "mere life," its death a "mere death."[16]

David Clark explores Heidegger's views in an exquisite and delicate essay. Heidegger famously, and unfathomably callously, connected animal deaths with genocide in a 1949 lecture, saying that the "'motorized food industry' was 'in essence the same as the manufacturing of corpses in gas chambers and extermination camps.'"[17] Clark advocates slow reading—an engagement with the text that finds nuances of meaning and avoids hasty judgments. There are more nuances to Heidegger's text than I am perhaps able to discern, but the clear, obvious, and catastrophic ethical thought here is to imply that humans who are destined for extinction by genocide also die mere deaths.

The idea that the death of an animal is incommensurate with the death of a human invites these kinds of terrible juxtapositions, and urges us to propose that no death is a mere death. And if animal deaths are not "mere," one way of understanding their fullness is through recollecting connectivity. The death of an animal creates a loss in the fabric of life, a loss that reverberates across other living beings, human and others.

In the Northern Territory, Aboriginal people remarked upon how the Victoria River people were mad about their dogs. In the Victoria River region, people remarked on how the Yarralin mob was mad about dogs. Every family has dogs. Formerly the dogs were all dingoes, but contemporary "camp dogs," as they are called, are a strange and fascinating mix of dog breeds, most of them of European origin. Each dog has a personal name, and many of the names are the names of Dreaming places in the person's own country. Dogs are fitted into the kinship system and addressed by name, nickname, or kin term.

Within Yarralin, people remarked upon how Old Tim was mad about his dogs. They laughed at his attachment to his dogs, and at the numbers of dogs in his entourage (sometimes claimed to be a hundred or more). Old Tim didn't seem to mind being laughed at; he loved his dogs, and respected them. His animal kin were dingoes, so he was a dog man, and was deeply committed to all dogs. The fact that he and his wife had no children may have contributed to his love of his dogs. But his attachment may also have been a response to earlier decades when Aboriginal people's dogs were massacred regularly. The police journals mention shooting dogs in utterly brief notes; there is, as far as I know, only one narratival account of "dog-shooting." The anthropologists R. and C. Berndt wrote a collection of vignettes about cattle-station life in the Victoria River District in the 1940s. They say that the narrated events are founded on fact, while the characters are fictitious. Here is a portion of their story about dog shooting, edited to take out repetitions but not to remove the ugly language which itself is part of the emotional energy of the account:

> Mounted Constable Guppy stopped his truck several yards from the camp. It was simpler that way, didn't give the niggers too much warning. . . . He slung his rifle over one shoulder and stepped briskly over to the humpies.
>
> "P'liceman! P'liceman!" The cry rang in fear through the camp.

They had seen him coming, but it was too late by then to rush their best dogs to safety among the bushes. . . . Frantically they tried to bundle their favourite dogs into the huts. And a few optimistic souls went racing for the scrub, holding some dogs at the end of long leashes, with others scampering beside them. M. C. Guppy smiled grimly to himself: good haul here, the beggars must've been breedin' 'em up since last time. He raised his rifle and sighted the flying figures.

Then pandemonium broke loose. As the bullets flew past them the women screamed in fright, dragging their animals ever faster behind them. A dog yelped suddenly, leapt into the air, and rolled kicking in the dust. Another followed, and another. One, hobbling off wounded in the shoulder was an easy mark; its body sagged on the leash, hampering its sobbing mistress for a second before she dropped the strap and fled panting. . . .

A group of old women cowered beneath a leafy shade, with a precious kangaroo dog concealed among them under a blanket. But the policeman knew all about such tricks. His bullet ploughed through the blanket to his quarry, singeing the white hair of one of its guardians so that they scattered in shrieking terror. . . .

One bullet struck the wall a couple of inches above the old man's head, where he lay groaning feebly in his canvas wrappings, . . . His oldest wife ran anxiously towards him and took him trembling in her arms. . . . A tear trickled down her withered cheeks. They shrank against the hut as the policeman strode past them, roughly pushing aside a dead dog with the toe of his polished boot.

Dogs were loping in all directions from the camp. Good, bad and indifferent, those that were valuable for hunting, those that were only mediocre, and those that were actively a nuisance: it made no difference. All were dogs, and all alike must fall before the rain of bullets. . . .

At last he put down his rifle and looked around him. No dogs in the camp now, only a bunch o' niggers scared half out o' their wits. Do 'em no end of good, show 'em what a policeman could do if he felt like it: useless bunch o' good-for-nothings.[18]

In another story that also involves a dog shooting, the authors imagine an Aboriginal woman's response in these words: "No, I don't want to think about it. It reminds me of the days when they used to shoot lots of people at once, not just one or two at a time; and I hate to think about that. Why, I might have been there myself."[19]

The use of dog shooting to induce terror, and thus to display power, is vivid in these passages. For people who had already been subjected to massacres, the dog shooting was a clear message of the right to kill with impunity. The power and terror show us a darker porosity to the West's human-animal boundary: one in which humans are animalized so as to be killed with impunity. We don't have to strain to understand the threat contained in dog shooting.

In the aftermath of the shooting, people buried their dogs. As we try to imagine these mass funerals we can almost hear the crying and the wailing, almost taste the hot, flowing tears. People were burying their kin, and as they did so they looked into a death space in which not only their loved ones, but the future generations of their loved ones had been exterminated. They were looking into an emptiness that used to be dogs, and this emptiness was not a departure that could be twisted back into life, but was rather a one-way trip into nowhere. This emptiness bore a message: there could be another emptiness, one that used to be people. And while people cried for the memory of their dogs, there would perhaps be no one left to cry for them. They were looking already into the possibility of their own extinction, and they knew they might descend into a death place out of which no voice or narrative could emerge.

The face of genocide and the face of extinction both disappear into a particularly deathful emptiness. Death is not turned back toward life, but rather becomes a journey of no return, an event with no future, a loss so absolute that terms like "nothingness" or "emptiness" seem wholly inadequate.

The beauty of death lies in its mystery. To see the light of life leave the eyes of a dying creature is to see briefly into a region that is unknown and unknowable. Unknowable, and unimaginable, and yet still intimate.

I learned to see the light disappear from the eyes of animals when I went hunting. Often an animal would look at us in the moment before it was shot. We saw it die; sometimes we had to finish it off with our bare hands. And then there was the distribution. When you cut into an animal, the thing that is so surprising is the reminder of how warm mammals are on the inside. You have your hands inside the animal, and you know without any doubt that the way this animal feels to your hands is exactly how you would feel if someone were doing this to you—the same heat, same textures, the fresh smell, the red blood. That intimacy of interchangeable interiority forms a special kind of empathy based on the tactile knowledge of our mammalian kinship and our shared condition as creatures born to die. This dead animal could be me, and I myself will one day be a dead animal.

The awareness is made more complex by the fact of eating. This animal would become part of my body, would sustain me and let me live another day. As I continue to live, my consciousness of death and blood continue in the world where this animal no longer lives. Within these tactile webs of immediacy, killing is part of life because death is part of life. To be alive is to know that one's life is dependent on the deaths of others. Those deaths are not abstractions but rather are touched and ingested throughout one's life.

Emmanuel Levinas tells us that from within an ethic of responsibility, the first commandment is "thou shalt not kill."[20] He was speaking of humans, leaving the question of killing animals open and unanswered. His perspective did not include hunter-gatherer peoples like Old Tim. As I think about Levinas and the idea of a first commandment, I imagine that if Old Tim and others had a set of commandments (which they don't), the comparable one would be "Thou shalt not turn thine eyes away from the deaths of animals."

Animal deaths within a kinship system are situated within relationships of accountability. In the first instance, one is accountable to the human relations of the animal, for it is they who will take direct action if their kin are being wronged, by overhunting, for example. More widely, however, every decision to kill an animal takes place within a wider set of relations signaled by the term "good country." The purpose of killing animals is to nurture humans; it is not to eradicate animals or to wreck country. Good country is a flourishing set of relationships—interdependent and mutual. The work that Aboriginal people do for life-in-country is embedded in ongoing relationships of care and nurturance. This is not to say that all actions are perfect, that mistakes are never made, or that individuals never run amok. It is to say that country is the living context in which past, present, and future are part of cross-species relationships of care.

The underlying logic of connectivity is important for what it has to say about self-interest. In the lifeworld of connectivity, the well-being of one is enmeshed in the well-being of others. There is no position outside of connection, and therefore what happens to one has effects on the well-being of others. There is immense vulnerability here, as one's own well-being is dependent on what happens to others, but at the same time there is resilience. To care for others is to care for one's self. There is no way to disentangle self and other, and therefore there is no self-interest that concerns only the self. Interests are mutual, and while they are not indistinguishable, they are situated within the larger dance of life which involves life *and* death, self *and* other, us *and* them.

Against such a system of entangled interests and accountability, we can juxtapose the indifference that philosophers such as Clark and Derrida identify as one of the many terrible consequences of thinking that there is a solid boundary between animals and humans. Clark writes of "the alibis that always put the human somewhere else, doing something else when it comes to killing animals and dehumanized or animalized humans: the 'culling' and 'management' of herds, the 'euthanization' of laboratory animals, but also the 'cleansing' and 'pacification' of human populations, the 'saving' of villages by their incineration."[21]

Words help disguise accountability, and so does the division of labor in segmented societies. In contrast to the tactile immediacy of killing and eating that brought us into a region of encounter, claim, and responsibility when we were hunting, our Western contexts do not offer many opportunities to see most of the deaths on which our lives depend, either directly or indirectly. These days hunting is the exception, not the rule, and it is so regulated by external authorities that it does not require a foundational understanding of connectivity and a capacity to be self-regulating (although individual hunters may indeed understand connectivity and regulate themselves). Those of us who purchase most of our food are implicated in contemporary animal farming, the mainstream methods of which involve an amplification of the monstrosity of animal deaths, a monstrosity expressed superbly by Derrida: "the industrialization of what can be called the production for consumption of animal meat, artificial insemination on a massive scale, more and more audacious manipulations of the genome, the reduction of the animal not only to production and overactive reproduction (hormones, genetic crossbreeding, cloning, and so on) of meat for consumption but also of all sorts of other end products, and all of that in the service of a certain being and the so-called human well-being of man."[22] We know about this monstrosity, but most of us don't experience it. We are outside the feedlot and the abattoir, and we know how to keep our distance.

Are extinctions so different? For the most part it is hard to make the connections that are necessary for understanding that extinctions are casualties of production for consumption. The industrialized manufacture of corpses for food is sustained at the expense of hundreds of thousands of other lives. Species, ecosystems, habitats, relationships, and connections that sustain the web of life on Earth become "collateral casualties" in the rush for consumption.[23] More often than not, monstrous cruelty and massive wastage are hidden within organized invisibility. We do get occasional glimpses of terrible, faraway processes of extinction: satellite imagery, for example, of polar bears struggling to survive on the disappearing ice. We cannot avoid knowing that we are implicated, that the loss of ice is a human-induced process as well. Regularly we read about animals that are facing extinction because they are being hunted to death for commercial purposes, or because their forest homes are being leveled, or because they are deemed to be pests. All too often, it seems, we manage to find "alibis" for being elsewhere.

Humanity's capacity for cruelty and self-insulation washes up against humanity's capacity for compassion, and very often finds a level marked by indifference or helplessness. How shall we see the eyes, the relationships, the companionship, the connections, the crossovers that connect their deaths with our lives? How shall we engage our imagination so as to reach into these death places?

3. Bobby's Face, My Love

I n 1975, Emmanuel Levinas wrote an essay called "Name of a Dog." It tells the story of an event that occurred during World War II, when he was a prisoner. During the Second World War, Levinas was living in Paris, having left his native Lithuania in order to pursue his intellectual life in France. He enlisted in the French army, and was captured and put to work in a forestry commando unit for Jewish prisoners of war in Nazi Germany.[1] There an event occurred that, within the confines and horrors of the prison camp, was close to miraculous. Levinas's work group was for a brief period adopted by a dog. They named him Bobby, and Bobby saw them off to work in the morning, greeting them with his wagging tail as they lined up. Bobby welcomed them back in the evening, excitedly barking when they came in. Levinas calls Bobby the last Kantian in Nazi Germany.[2]

The essay was written thirty years later; it is a curious work, never to be adequately understood, I believe, and composed implicitly, perhaps, as homage to the dog. In David Clark's beautiful words, it is an essay "written out in Bobby's long shadow."[3] This strangely provocative essay had the disheartening effect of convincing me of the intractability of Levinas's commitment to abstract boundaries. I have drawn inspiration from Levinas in much of my work, and this is possible because I have been working with a minority reading.[4] Levinas's great contribution, in this reading, is to pull ethics away from abstractions and to locate ethical call-and-response within the living reality of the material world. Levinas does not say this precisely, but in saying that ethics precedes self, that ethics is that which calls us into relationship, one logical conclusion is that we are called into becoming. Each becoming is historically situated and open to others, and is thus unique. Becoming is always grounded in the specifics of life; it is not, and cannot be, an abstraction.

The problem is that at the same time that Levinas writes so lovingly of Bobby, he says that dogs are without ethics and without logos (152), thus reasserting an absolute boundary between himself and Bobby. Even worse, perhaps, he writes that Bobby was "without the brain needed to universalise maxims and drives" (153). These nine words appear to unmake most of what a minority reading treasures in this great philosopher. The essay is odd, tender, provocative, and mysterious, and has been analyzed by many scholars.[5] Llewellyn's reference to becoming obsessed with Bobby states my condition as well; it is almost impossible to stop circling questions of who (man or dog) in this essay philosophizes, who recognizes and attests to the dignity of whom, why anyone would want to claim to universalize, whether the inability to universalize is being praised or denigrated, and who, at the end of the day, is silent.

On the face of it, Levinas rejects Bobby. Llewellyn explains: "We can be under an obligation only to a being with whom we can be . . . face to face. In the very human world of Emmanuel Kant, the other man is the only being with whom I come face to face. So too in the very human world of Emmanuel Levinas. The only face we behold is the human face and that is the only face to which we are beholden. Ethically that is all that matters."[6] I experience a wave of anguish every time I think about Levinas's rejection of Bobby, and so do others. David Clark, for example, writes in his stunning essay, "What is 'language' if it is not the wagging of a tail, and 'ethics' if it is not the ability to greet one another and to dwell together *as* others?"[7] In another fascinating essay, Peter Steeves addresses Bobby's lack of face: "What could Bobby be missing: Is his snout too pointy to constitute a face? Is his nose too wet? Do his ears hang low; do they wobble to and fro? How can this *not* be a face?"[8]

"Name of a Dog" goes to the heart of how Western thought has defined humanity. One of the main boundaries in Western thought that separates humanity from other living things is the boundary between humans and other animals.[9] Levinas's rejection of Bobby is anguishing because the greatest twentieth-century philosopher of ethical alterity could not unambiguously make a place in his ethics for the one living being who approached him and others with full recognition of their humanity. Other sources of anguish arise. Elie Wiesel's famous insight reveals the relationship between the Holocaust and the Enlightenment. He writes that at Auschwitz not only man died; the Idea of Man died as well.[10] Levinas, writing thirty years later, reinstates the Idea of Man. Against the realities of this time, these encounters, these awful uncertainties and disastrous cruelties, Levinas drew boundaries that inscribed abstract and universal categories. His ability to universalize his maxims constitutes the overturning of what I have taken to be his radical contribution to philosophy, and restores the tyranny of the abstract over the living reality of the world. Levinas takes logos to be that which fundamentally differentiates humans from animals. He thus reinscribes the big dualisms of Western thought—mind over and above matter, the abstract and eternal over the living reality in all its immediacy, proximity, and dynamic transience.

In retracing this boundary he was, arguably, promoting a type of vision that was also central to Nazism. Zygmunt Bauman writes that in genocide people are killed for what they are, not for what they have done. Nothing people can do will alter the sentence of death, not submission, not rebellion, not affection, not anything. He concludes, "The stoutly monological character of genocide, this resolute pre-emption of all dialogue, this prefabricated asymmetry of relationship, this one-sidedness of authorship and actorship alike is, I propose, the most decisive constitutive feature of all genocide."[11] I am not suggesting that Levinas was promoting genocide. Indeed, one of the astounding aspects of "Name of a Dog" is his daring willingness to suggest close parallels between animals who are killed with impunity and humans who are killed with impunity.[12] What I find so catastrophic is his replication of the structure that underlies the possibility of genocide, most particularly, the boundary determined in advance, and therefore unable to be responsive to specificities; and thus his valuing of the boundary over and above the living reality. There was nothing Bobby could have done to penetrate the barrier Levinas erected.

Silent Dogs

Levinas's discussion of Bobby also works with biblical texts, drawing on two brief appearances of dogs in Exodus. The first, Exodus 11:6–7, concerns God's foretelling of the night when He will stalk Egypt in the form of Death, killing every firstborn person and animal among the Egyptians, and delivering the Israelites from servitude. The relevant passage is interestingly complex. It is part of a conversation between Moses and Pharaoh, and it is important in looking at the brief text to remember that this is the seventh such conversation. On each previous occasion, Moses has foretold a disaster for Egypt unless Pharaoh lets the Israelites go free. On each occasion, God intervenes to harden Pharaoh's heart so that he refuses, and each refusal is followed by the promised disaster. In the passage Levinas discusses, the words are spoken by Moses to Pharaoh, and Moses says that he is reporting what the Lord had told him, so the words can be read as God addressing Pharaoh: "And there shall be a loud cry in all the land of Egypt such as has never been or will ever be again; but not a dog shall snarl at any of the Israelites, at man or beast—in order that you may know that the Lord makes a distinction between Egypt and Israel."[13]

Levinas finds in God's actions the opening up of a clear path toward freedom and dignity. The dogs' silence is, in Levinas's analysis, a form of communication. Dogs, he says, will attest both to human freedom and canine dignity. He takes this event to be the reason for the second passage he works with. Exodus 22:30 has as its context a long set of laws being delivered to the people by Moses while they are in the desert. One of the laws reads as follows (again, God is addressing people through Moses): "You shall be holy people to Me: you must not eat flesh torn by beasts in the field; you shall cast it to the dogs." Dogs were allowed to scavenge; humans were not. According to Levinas, this passage poses a paradox: Why would animals be given rights, in this case the right to this particular meat? And he answers: because they have borne witness, "there is transcendence in the animal." And the analysis goes deeper, seeming to suggest that dogs can transform cast-off flesh into "good flesh" because of their "direct thoughts."[14] It seems that their lack of logos is also their privilege, and further, that on the night of the Exodus they, too, had a place in the divine story.

Approaching these passages from another perspective, I find a different story, one that is not unfamiliar. Let us go back to the one time the dogs did not bark in the night. Recall that the Israelites had been instructed to make sacrifice and to daub the blood on the doorposts and lintels of their homes. It is impossible to imagine the horrors of this night, but we know that God's deathwork descends into homes, fields, and byres, bloody and implacable. In the midst of all this terror, the Israelites flee Egypt forever. They are not going secretly; the Egyptians are begging them to leave. They run off with what they can carry of wealth, both their own and that of the Egyptians, going into the night, among the screams, the wails, the myriad grieving sounds of loss; they flee with their children, their animals, their gold and silver, making their way out of Egypt in fear and haste. And not a single dog growls or attacks them as they rush through the night. Through city streets and along fields and pastures they travel as strangers, and the dogs are silent. Everyone would have known that God had commandeered them to his will, and his will that night included terror. As Steeves points out, God forced the dogs into silence, and so the dogs did God's work that night, but at the cost of their own voice.

Not only does God repress the dogs' canine capacities, he also homogenizes them. Through this night of grief and fear strode the destroyer. Had they not been silenced, some dogs would have voiced the howling lamentation they raise in response to death. Others would have fled, barking like mad, only to become lost and never to return home. No doubt others would have run around in circles yapping for hours, and still others would have slunk into the kitchen and hidden quivering behind the cupboard. Dog personalities and diversities were suppressed to conform to an image of snarling, and the snarl was suppressed. The subsequent law asserting that dogs, but not people, shall eat carrion meat, again reinstates boundaries and, perforce, homogenizes the beings on both sides.

I find myself somewhat baffled in trying to understand why the silence of the Egyptians' dogs was deemed by God to be a message of which Pharaoh would take particular notice. Perhaps God, who, it must be recalled, was terribly keen to prove his power to Pharaoh, anticipated a contest not only between himself and Pharaoh, but between his people's dogs and the Egyptian people's dogs. Perhaps he expected that when Pharaoh heard the sounds of terror, he would seek protection from his dog, and then he would find that even the royal Pharaohnic dog was silent in that terrible night.

The structure of God's action is the structure Bauman identifies as the constitutive feature of genocide: classification on the basis of who people are rather than what they have done. God made and enforced the boundaries between life and death: death to the firstborn of all Egyptian people and animals, life and liberation for the Israelites. Here God foreshadows the genocidal action he will pursue when he brings his people into the Promised Land, as Regina Schwartz discusses in detail in her study of "the violent legacy of monotheism."[15]

So it seems that God had views on the drawing of boundaries of lifeworthiness. The chosen people will be rescued; the rest will suffer or die. In relation to Levinas's treatment of Bobby, we see a parallel structure—an ethics-worthiness boundary. The boundary determines who is worthy of ethical response and who is not. For me, the most tortured aspect of this story of violence is the silence. In Exodus the dogs are silenced, and their very silence becomes their testimony. They were set up by God as being incapable of witnessing without God's intervention, and the erasure of their voices becomes their fate: in their own being they are not good enough. Their testimony is both to God's power and their own inadequacy. Levinas gives us a similar story in his analysis of Bobby. First Bobby is silenced by the decree that he is without logos; then his silence is used to exclude him from the domain of ethics-worthiness.

If, as I argue, there is violence in generating categories, homogenizing diversity, and squashing living beings into homogenized categories, then am I perhaps undertaking the same violent operation with God? For that matter, is Levinas? It can be argued that God, too, is more diverse than he appears in the Exodus story. Sometimes he breathes life into his creation; sometimes he wipes out his creation. Literary analysis indicates two accounts of God in the Bible, indicating two narrative strands that, rather than being reconciled, are set side by side.[16] In contrast, the noted theologian Joseph Soloveitchik argues that the doubling up is not a product of different narratives, but rather is an account of dual character. He looks at this duality in the context of the two creation stories in Genesis, and concludes that there are two stories of creation because humans have a dual nature. The first, which he calls Adam (1), results from God's work creating Adam and Eve in his image and authorizing them to take dominion over the Earth; the second, Adam (2), is created from clay, and is brought into life by God's own breath.[17] If, for the sake of encountering God's complexity, we accept that humans have a dual character, may we not also propose that God has a dual character? One character, amply attested to in sacred texts, is the God (1) of extremes: creating, but also punishing, destroying, terrorizing. The other, God (2), often hidden, is most beautifully discernable in songs of praise; he is a good shepherd.

Returning to the Exodus, let us imagine that while God (1), the Angel of Death, walks the land, God (2) arrives with his rod and staff, to take charge of the departure. He whistles up the Israelites' dogs and forms them into teams whose task is to get their households out of Egypt. These people, we might recall, this "rabble from the house of slavery" as Yehuda Amichai calls them,[18] have been slaves for four hundred years. Now, suddenly, they are meant to organize a mass departure. One can imagine everyone tripping over everyone else, bumping into each other, and making a complete mess of it. The good shepherd sets the pace, and he asks all the other dogs, just this once, to remain silent in order not to panic the people. Anyone who has seen sheep being pushed into a situation that is new to them and in which they feel uncertain knows how stupidly unresponsive they become when they are frightened or flustered. The Israelites' dogs will facilitate the Exodus in their own doglike ways. They'll round up the Israelites, nipping at their heels, harrying the stragglers and gathering in the strays. The good shepherd and his dogs watch over the flock, ensuring that they neither stumble nor stray.

This reimagining of the story differs from Levinas's account, although it also alludes to another daring aspect of Levinas's essay: his brush with the hint of closeness between God and dog. In my God (2) version, the dogs are testifying to the human potential for mayhem. It is the collaborative work of the dogs that enables Israel to be delivered from the land of Pharaoh. And while I have not attempted to engage directly with the second text on eating carrion, there is a line of analysis that speaks to the condition of coming out of slavery. In this analysis, the forty years in the wilderness were required for a generation to mature who had grown up with no experience of slavery. Rules about people not eating carrion seem to fit well in this analysis. The implication is that dogs know already what they can eat; people need to be told.

But perhaps I am squashing Levinas into too narrow a vision. There may be two sides to Levinas as well. His account of the dogs' right to eat carrion asserts that it is the purity (the absence of the complications of logos) that enables them to transform contaminated meat into their own friendly flesh. In this and a few other sentences, Levinas adds complications and paradoxes to his comments on dogs. Levinas (1) rejects Bobby in the end, in order to hold on to a universalizable ethics. Levinas (2) reveals very little of himself in the essay. A possible reading asks: Did Levinas (2) seek to escape his own abstractions by situating himself with the dog, rather than with the humans? Is he advocating the proposition that Bobby's call delivers us from the tyranny of abstractions? Does his slightly jocular tone of voice overlay a hiddenness and silence that are messages in themselves? I return to this last question in chapter 9.

Levinas's "Name of a Dog" adds a complicating twist to Michael Soulé's view that people save what they love. There seems to be no doubt that the POWs loved Bobby, and yet Levinas seems to have rejected him. The fact that this boundary between humans and animals is sustained even in the face of love poses a terrible question that is exposed brilliantly by Nobel laureate J. M. Coetzee in his novel *Disgrace.* This prize-winning book is extremely complex, and my reading works with only one of its strands. My proposition is that one narrative woven into *Disgrace* is an account of Levinas and Bobby, an analysis of "Name of a Dog" in fictional form.

The main character in *Disgrace* is a middle-aged man named David Lurie. In the beginning of the book, he is a university lecturer whose specialty is Romantic poetry. He suffers numerous falls from grace and eventually tumbles into a position as an assistant in an animal welfare clinic. The clinic is underfunded (animals are not a state funding priority), and the main role is to hold them for a while in the hopes of adoption, and then to kill them. David's role is first to care for dogs and then to assist in the killing, taking the dogs into the death room, and then disposing of the bodies.

The dogs are killed on Sundays, and the incinerator does not open until Monday. David finds he cannot simply dump the dead bodies at the refuse site overnight, nor can he leave them to the brutalities of the men who work the incinerator. Those men struggle with the dogs' rigor mortis, and hammer the bodies into manageable shapes. David takes the dead bodies home, and then takes them to the incinerator and puts them into the machinery with his own hands. Why, he asks himself, does he go to this trouble? Not for the dogs, since they are dead, "and what do dogs know of honour and dishonour anyway?" he asks himself. He concludes that he does it for himself, for his idea of a world "in which men do not beat corpses into a more convenient shape for processing."[19]

The parallels with the Nazi genocide are compelling, especially when one considers that parallels between animal and human holocausts are a recurring theme in Coetzee's work. Coetzee always resists uncomplicated readings, and the Nazi parallels are never allowed to stabilize. Still, they raise the question of lifeworthiness. David and the vet in charge of the clinic, Bev, make these life-or-death decisions every Sunday, and they see their work as an outcome of social indifference: the dogs die because nobody wants them. Coetzee uses the word *Lösung* in this context, the Nazi term for the "solution" (218).[20]

The solution for dogs is a question for God. Is this what God does? Does he make lifeworthiness decisions and process humans and others through the death room? The Exodus story says "yes"; Coetzee takes away the narrative of deliverance, and says "yes." In fact, *Disgrace* reflects the Exodus story in perfect mirrored imagery. In Exodus, the chosen people are delivered—that is the point of the story. In *Disgrace,* the unchosen are disposed of—and that is the point of the story. The unchosen are exactly that, and nothing they can do will save them.

Coetzee says that death is a disgrace. He is quite explicit. When David starts to assist with the killing, he learns that the dogs do not want to go into the death room: "They flatten their ears, they droop their tails, as if they too feel the disgrace of dying; locking their legs, they have to be pulled or pushed or carried over the threshold" (143). But what is the disgrace? This is the central question. In reading *Disgrace* as the story of Levinas and Bobby, my attention keeps returning to David. It is difficult to convey what an empty character he is. Coetzee describes his emptying this way:

> He has a sense that, inside him, a vital organ has been bruised, abused—perhaps even his heart. For the first time he has a taste of what it will be like to be an old man, tired to the bone, without

hopes, without desires, indifferent to the future. . . . [H]e feels his
interest in the world draining from him drop by drop. It may take
weeks, it may take months before he is bled dry, but he is bleeding.
When that is finished he will be like a fly-casing in a spiderweb,
brittle to the touch, lighter than rice-chaff, ready to float away. (107)

Into this emptying husk of a man a dog intrudes. A young, crippled
male dog at the clinic arouses David's feelings, and offers him affection: "[The dog] is not 'his' in any sense; he has been careful not to
give it a name . . . nevertheless, he is sensible of a generous affection streaming out toward him from the dog. Arbitrarily, uncondi-
tionally, he has been adopted; the dog would die for him, he knows"
(215). We are almost at the end of the book when this happens, and
we cannot evade the terrible premonition that somehow the dog
is going to die for David. I cannot write about him in a nameless
state, and so I am offering him a name: Youngfella. He is a dog who
frisks when he is let out of his cage, who wants to love and wants to
live, who knows how to play, and knows how to invite friendship.
He calls forth affection, and pulls at the heart. David becomes fond
of him. And yet Youngfella is doomed to be killed because nobody
wants him.

On the last killing day in the book, David saves Youngfella until
last, but in the end he goes and opens the cage door and calls the
dog. "The dog wags its crippled rear, sniffs his face, licks his cheeks,
his lips, his ears. He does nothing to stop it." "Come," he says, and
carries the dog into the death room "in his arms like a lamb." Bev
asks if he is giving him up. Yes, he says, "I am giving him up" (220).

We are clearly in the presence of sacrifice. But why is Youngfella
disposable? Levinas gave up Bobby to save the Idea of Man. What
does David save in giving up Youngfella? On the face of it, David is
sacrificing the dog in order to save *both* the boundary between human and animal *and* human control over that boundary. His choice
furthers his infectious emptiness. This was his last fall into disgrace:
he could save the dead bodies from dishonor, but he would not save
the one creature who adored and adopted him. We see, then, that
he is more crippled than Youngfella, and afflicted with his own rigor
mortis of the soul. Coetzee tells us that disgrace is not in the dying,
although it lingers in that region. Youngfella's fate is quite horribly

that of being killed because no one will include you in the world of life and love. The disgrace arises in that rejection: because all your love, and all your caresses, your face, your tongue, your happy barking, none of that is enough to call a human into relationship. This turning away is David's disgrace.

The Eleventh Question

The French feminist philosopher Luce Irigaray poses ten "Questions for Levinas." One by one, they spotlight the devastating emptiness she finds in his work. The emptiness hinges on Levinas's dedication to the abstract; he denies the real-world specific presence of others, generating a wholly abstract Other. Levinas works with images—face, caress, call—that are embodied and tactile, of the flesh and of the world. And yet, he plucks them from contact with material referents, reworking them into abstractions. He has written that "The best way of encountering the Other is not even to notice the color of his eyes!"[21] Irigaray's question in a nutshell is: Where is the specificity of women's difference if the other is always already gendered? This, of course, is Irigaray's main project: to claim a subjectivity that is embodied, sensuous, specific, and inclusive. She does not confine herself to human others, but also questions Levinas's avoidance of "the face of the natural universe."[22] For Irigaray, the embodiment of human specificity is inextricable from the embodiment of the world.

Levinas and Irigaray agree that ethics should provide the foundation for philosophy.[23] Where they differ is over the specificity of the other. Levinas wants to efface difference; Irigaray maintains that a system of intersubjective ethics cannot rest on erasure. This is a thorny issue, and I return to it again in chapter 9. For now, let us stay with Irigaray and her loving but critical insight. She shows that erasure is a form of violence, a denial of the reality of others. Through her questions, we see that the philosopher of ethical alterity actually erases the other, sacrificing her specificity and embodied caress. Irigaray's questions expose this operation: the erasure of the specificity of others is a form of silencing that withers the fullness of the self while obviating the presence of others. The startling secret she exposes is that there is no "other" in Levinas.

Levinas's essay could have gone differently. He might have given us an ecological ethics that brought us into interspecies relationships, and into love and into connectivity. Bobby could have led him there: Bobby did not offer abstractions. He jumped and barked, and no doubt licked the men's hands and faces. He was not addressing the Idea of Man or man marked by some species-specific dignity, but rather real men, prisoners, men who were doomed under Nazi rule and were saved only by the Allied victory. These were men who would die, or would live to become famous philosophers, not because of an Idea, but through the unpredictable contingencies of history. Against the reality of Bobby, Levinas chose an abstract ethic which is empty in itself and which empties the world through its silencing and its refusals.

To consider the possibility of a different story is to raise yet another question for Levinas, this one concerning God. This is the eleventh question: Is it possible ethically to embrace both? To embrace the God who stalks the land choosing, rejecting, and killing, and at the same time to embrace the dog who enters the Nazi death world wagging his tail and offering his beautiful enthusiasm for life? Levinas seems to say "no" to the eleventh question, sacrificing Bobby not only to save an Idea of Man, but also to save an Idea of God. This is God (1), saved, it seems, so as to go on exercising the authority of the boundary dividing those who will live from those who will die, those whose appeal is heeded and those who are refused. To commit to God (1) is to refuse even to save those one loves, if they are on the wrong side of the boundary.[24]

David Lurie offered more and more sacrifice, more killing, and turned the killing into more explicit forms of sacrifice. As with Abraham, the toughest sacrifice is of someone or something you love. As Coetzee shows us so clearly, love makes sacrifice an excruciating task. The story is ancient: Abraham was saved from having to kill his son. Having offered obedience to God, he was given an alternative: the ram appeared and was sacrificed. This story is often read against the context of other religions in the region in which human sacrifice was acceptable. On this reading, part of the special relationship between God and Abraham is that Abraham and his people do not sacrifice humans. From the perspective of the perilous boundary between humans and animals, we would keep the ram in the story. Then we would have to suggest that God values *human lives,* and values *animal deaths.* We would remember, then, that Kant and other human-focused philosophers held that the full transcendence of the human requires the sacrifice of the animal. We might think back to Exodus and remember that God values the lives of some humans, not all humans, and we would see a kind of logic for why people who are to be killed with impunity can be thought of as animals and as a kind of sacrifice in search of a better world. And of course we would always want to remember that those whom God claims to love stand with him on the life side of the boundary. As Jacques Derrida reminds us, "Even animals know . . . what is about to happen to them when man says 'Here I am' to God."[25]

Did David imagine that with his sacrifice he could fill his own emptiness? On behalf of Bobby, and Youngfella, and all the unchosen, Coetzee affirms: You could turn the whole world into a pile of ashes through sacrifice, but as you kill your fellow Earth creatures, you make yourself and the whole world more lonely, more empty, than when you started.

Emptiness leaves behind many darknesses. Bobby's long shadow extends from a Nazi death camp to our current moment of cascading loss of animals and plants, and it continues to communicate the truth of ethical proximity. Neither chosen nor un-chosen, but companions and participants, Bobby and all the dogs of deliverance bring us into encounter with the joy of the world, situated in the sounds, smells, and touch of the myriad living things. In such dramas of encounter and recognition we find ourselves becoming creatures who are recognized, and we are captured by the cool, dark beauty of a dog's nose, the warm rough-tongued caress, and the mystery that gazes back from the depths of a dog's eyes.

4. Ecological Existentialism

We are brothers and sisters of the world. Doesn't matter if you're bird, snake, fish, kangaroo: One Red Blood.—David Gulpilil, *Gulpilil: One Red Blood*, 2007

Ecological existentialism responds to the two big shifts in Western thought that define our current moment: the shift into uncertainty and the shift into connectivity. I will take a whirlwind tour through these shifts, with Lev Shestov, Ilya Prigogine, and Val Plumwood as guides. The tour is in response to Soulé's idea that people save what they love; the purpose is to ask: What is this "people" he's talking about?

Lev Shestov was an early critic of modernity and an advocate of existential philosophy. Born in 1866 in Russia, Shestov was educated there, and stayed there until 1895, when he began to travel in western Europe, living sometimes in Russia and sometimes in Germany or Switzerland. After the revolution, he emigrated to Paris, where he wrote and taught. As his work was translated into French, he became a key figure in both religious philosophy and existential philosophy, and had particular influence on Camus' thinking.[1] Shestov's thought works in two major directions. The first is his critique of modernity, focusing on its devotion to progress, certainty, and destiny. The second is his fierce commitment to a kind of "craziness"—a wild and daring wisdom—that calls for humanity to be in connection with the world. Within all his work is a powerful moral sensibility that calls for commitment, daring, and connectedness in the midst of uncertainty.

Shestov's sense of impending disaster was prophetic. In one of his most pungent passages, he says that the West's commitment to abstractions and certainty "would poison the joy of existence and lead men, through terrible and loathsome trails, to the threshold of nothingness."[2] In the context of his writing and his time, this is a statement of how the West was driving itself into existential despair. Perhaps already he was seeing the path of genocide that the Nazis were opening up. Now we can read it also as an ecological statement of how we are driving ourselves and our world into an ever-expanding death space.

"Existentialism" is a term with diverse connotations, a "much used, much disputed term."[3] I use it in a general way to indicate the key proposition that there is no predetermined essence of humanity, no ultimate goal toward which we are heading, and that we experience what appear to be astonishingly open ways of being and becoming human. My use of the term is clearly situated within the intellectual history that asks what humanity is and can be. The humanistic existential philosophers ascribed a terrible loneliness to humanity's freedom, a condition that arises because, in their view, we humans are effectively alone in the universe. The modern Western sense of human loneliness was perhaps kick-started with Copernicus, and was massively enhanced by scientific research that expanded the timeline of Earth and the universe. One effect of these expansions of time and decentering of Earth as the focus of the universe was to shrink the apparent significance of humanity. Jonas quotes Pascal, a Christian thinker of the seventeenth century: "Cast into the infinite immensity of spaces of which I am ignorant, and which know me not, I am frightened." In Jonas's view, it is the "know me not" part of the statement, the sense of cosmic indifference, that accelerates human loneliness.[4] Similarly, Soloveitchik, a twentieth-century Jewish thinker, offers a beautifully articulate expression of human loneliness in relation to time. He likens "man" to "a hitch-hiker suddenly invited to get into a swiftly traveling vehicle which emerged from nowhere and from which he will be dropped into the abyss of timelessness while the vehicle will rush on into parts unknown, continually taking on new passengers and dropping off old ones."[5]

Existentialism, never unified, and never given definitive boundaries, arises with the absence or death of God. With no god, and with a culture of dualistic thinking that separates humanity from all else on Earth, and with the loss of certainty and destiny that inheres in mechanistic worldviews, existential thought struggled with dread in the face of cosmic isolation. I modify the term "existentialism" with the term "ecological." Against existentialist loneliness, I propose that our condition as a co-evolving species of life on Earth, our kinship in the great family of life on Earth, situates us in time and place. We are still creatures for whom there is no predetermined essence or destiny; we are a work-in-progress. At the same time, as creatures enmeshed within the connectivities of Earth life, there is no ultimate isolation; we are thoroughly entangled. If there is loneliness, it is of our own making, as we saw with Bobby and Youngfella. In truth our lives are interspecies projects through and through.[6] Ecological existentialism thus proposes a kinship of becoming: no telos, no deus ex machina to rescue us, no clockwork to keep us ticking along; and on the other hand, the rich plenitude, with all its joys and hazards, of our entanglement in the place, time, and multispecies complexities of life on Earth.

Uncertainty: The Spectre of Mystery

For several millennia, the West has been in the grip of a deep desire for order, certainty, and predictability. The classical worldview lays out a template that has been reworked over several millennia: the whole is prior to the parts. If we think of a human being as a part of the larger whole which is prior to it, the implications are that the whole is better than the parts, since each part is only an incomplete fragment of the whole, and therefore the parts exist for the sake of the whole. As the whole precedes the parts, so the parts find the meaning of their existence by considering the whole. Order, predictability, and the possibility of comprehending it all are part of the thinking that is entailed with the proposition that the whole is prior to the parts. Shestov explains this in detail in the context of speculative philosophy:

> The essence and the meaning of the very concept of "speculation"—of "mental sight"—consists in man training himself to see in himself a part of the single whole and convincing himself that the meaning of his existence, his "destiny," consists in adapting his life to the being of the whole uncomplainingly and even joyously. A machine has screws, wheels, driving belts, etc. But both the people out of whom the universe arises as well as the individual parts out of which the machine is formed have no meaning in and of themselves. The meaning of their existence lies only in that the "whole"—the machine in the first instance, the world in the latter—should function

without impediment and move forward uninterruptedly in the direction established once and for all.[7]

In Plato's time, the order of the stars was the model of orderliness, and because there is order, the possibility of complete knowledge exists. Such knowledge would be gained through the use of abstract reason. In the *Phaedrus*, Plato wrote of a site beyond the distant starry skies which is the abode of reality: "It is there that true being dwells, without colour or shape, that cannot be touched; reason alone, the soul's pilot, can behold it, and all true knowledge is knowledge thereof."[8] He thus connects truth and true being with the abstract and immutable, with that which has no body, with an external standpoint far from Earth, and with the human faculty of reason. All of this is well outside the world of earthly materiality. The consolation of philosophy for Plato is to offer meaning that is accessible to man's reason and that transcends all that is finite and subject to change.

If the principles and rules are to be reliable, they must always be right, and in order for rules and principles always to be right, the cosmos itself must be unchanging. That which has been observed must hold true into the future as well. The correlation between past and future is known as time symmetry, and it requires immutability. Within the template of whole and part, and its correlated time symmetry, the living world of transience and flux is very much a poor relation.

Shestov's desire was to draw out the many and terrible implications of eternal and immutable "Certainty" (with a capital *C*):

Certainty kills God, because it denies God's own freedom to intervene in the world unpredictably;

Certainty dismisses the passionate and vivid qualities of life on earth because these qualities are mutable, sustained in flux, subject to death and fraught with uncertainty;

Certainty calls us to renounce our own selfhood, on the same grounds;

Certainty calls us to "renounce the world and that which is in the world" on the same grounds—that the world is transient, subject to death and fraught with uncertainty.[9]

The Certainty position is: "Everything that exists in the world passes away, is condemned to disappear. Is it worth the trouble to hold on to such a world?"[10] He suggests that in becoming slaves of Certainty, our understanding of our real place in the real world was seriously damaged, and the actual real world of our lives and deaths lost for us its "charm and fascination."[11]

Already, within Shestov's lifetime, Western thought was shaking its own foundations. We have reached "the end of certainty," in Ilya Prigogine's memorable phrase, and so we have reached the scientific end of millennia of thought. The methods of certainty have uncovered fundamental uncertainties in the cosmos and within Earth and life, and we are in the midst of a scientific upheaval that is more of a tsunami than a respectable little blip.

The new understanding reverses the whole-part relationship. Science is now asserting that the whole is greater than the sum of its parts. This is an absolute bombshell of an idea, defused to some degree by having become a cliché, but nevertheless of profound significance. The dream of complete certainty is a major casualty, and was expressed delightfully by Frank Egler: "Ecosystems may not only be more complex than we think, they may be more complex than we *can* think."[12] One cannot remove one's self from the system under examination; Plato's dream of a faraway site of pure knowledge is untenable. Because one is a part of the system, and because the system is always coming into being through the actions of the parts, the whole remains outside the possibility of one's comprehension.[13] The shift entails change from concepts of equilibrium to pervasive disequilibrium; from concepts of objectivity to intersubjectivity; from visions of deterministic prediction to an awareness of uncertainty and probability.[14]

With uncertainty, time symmetry is broken. It is not possible to assert that what has been observed in the past will always and necessarily hold good in the future. An impressive effect of the breaking of time symmetry is that mystery is brought back into human thought as an essential element of our lives, a part of thought rather than an enemy to be vanquished. We are not parts of the machine, but rather are participants in processes by which life is always coming into connectivity. As the whole is unknowable in its totality, so mystery becomes part of our human condition.

Ilya Prigogine's work has been with the time-dependent irreversible processes that are characteristic of life and that are far from equilibrium. Irreversible processes produce entropy, and they are well expressed through the metaphor of time's arrow. There is no way to turn back time, life leads into death, and there is no alternative. Prigogine's great scientific contribution is to show that the arrow of time is also a source of order: there is a constructive role, too, for irreversible time, since living things come into life as well as die. The same quality of irreversibility leads both to life and death, and thus life and death are mutually interactive.[15] Like Shestov, Prigogine maintains (and furthermore is able to prove mathematically) that the complexity of the real world is founded in the transience and flux of life and death.

The humanist existentialism of the last century mirrored this shift, rejecting attempts to build philosophy on the basis of the idea that the meaning of being human is embedded in cosmic certainties. Without certainty, the long history of thought that drew its logical, metaphorical, and mystical power from the idea of the whole is overturned, and we are thrown back on what existential philosophy has called the Absurd. In this world of uncertainty, nothing is guaranteed. There is no future point of perfection toward which all is moving, and there is no whole that directs us.

Connectivity: The Spectre of Animals

Animals haunt the Western imagination, a haunting entailed by and sustained through our long-standing, but now crumbling, dualisms. Dualistic thought, pervading the ancient world of the West and continuing to this day, requires two intellectual moves: separation and hierarchy. The great eco-feminist philosopher Val Plumwood uses the term "hyperseparation" to describe this kind of divide.[16] Hyperseparation not only says that things are different, it says that the difference is oppositional and extreme. Thus, for example, where men are taken to be rational, women must be emotional; if men are active, women must be passive; if men are hard, women must be soft. The hyperseparated dualisms link up: if humans are rational, nature must be mindless; if humans are active, nature must be passive. If humans think and speak, animals must be dumb brutes. Mind is imagined to be over and above matter, cosmos or heaven is deemed to be over and above earth, eternity and certainty are valued over and above transience, mutability, and uncertainty, and so on. The hierarchy of superiority is also a hierarchy of control: culture over nature, mind over matter, and so on and on in the most familiar and oppressive fashion.

A major dualism is that between "culture" and "nature." Culture refers to human beings, and nature refers to all the rest of the living world that is not human. Nature/culture is a divide between humans and the rest that sets the human over and above all else. Within this binary, the separation between humans and animals is crucial, since animals are those parts of nature closest to us in face, form, and function. Questions arise: If we are like them, do we lose our sense of having a unique origin and destiny? If we are not like them, are we isolated? If we do not belong with them, with whom do we belong? To whom are we accountable? Where are the boundaries of our ethics? Where are the boundaries of life, death, thought, experience, knowledge, empathy, concern, intelligence, communication, love? Who are we when we are with them, and then again, who are we without them?

Kinship: The Spectre of Connectivity

In our new knowledge system, the world is not finished. Our human species is evolved from and always involved in world making. This does not mean that we humans are all-powerful or all-knowing. Far from it. Our power exceeds our capacity to contain its effects, and thus we are constantly confronted with our own powerlessness. Our knowledge is necessarily and forever incomplete. The world—the living Earth—is always making itself, and we are part of that process, both made by the world and part of its continuous making. In short, we are participants in its ongoing story.

Life is a process of becoming, and thus we face more questions. Does the natural world have its own desires, its own memories, goals, and sentience? The biologists Lynn Margulis and Dorion Sagan say "yes" to these questions. Life, they tell us, is "matter that chooses. Each living being . . . responds sentiently to a changing environment and tries during its life to alter itself."[17] With choice, life systems are full of unpredictability and uncertainty, and while it is not the case that absolutely anything can happen and survive, in its ongoing self-organization and self-repair, the organism, or the eco-system, or even the whole biosphere, is working with the uncertain-ties of change and striving to sustain its own flourishing. We can say that life has desires, and we can talk about what these desires are: life desires complexity, life wants to join, create, experiment, do more.

Where humanistic existentialism found humanity isolated in the face of the cosmos, new understandings of life's connectivity tell us that in fact we are not alone. We are in a world of intersubjectiv-ity—a world in which sentient subjects face each other. The Danish biologist Jesper Hoffmeyer takes the understanding of intersubjec-tivity to a glorious extreme. He contends that all that exists is based entirely on communication. The universe, he says, is a semiosphere. Subjectivity is necessary to life, and indeed is necessary to the whole cosmos. "Life is based entirely on semiosis, on sign opera-tions." Hoffmeyer restores connectivity through an examination of semiotic processes that work across scales from cosmos, to Earth, to living systems, and to individuals. That we seem to work with the same basic desires as all other systems is not an anthropomorphic projection, as is often argued. Recent work, Hoffmeyer's and that of numerous others, shows that the connectivities, similarities, and parallels are real, and thus comprehensibility too is a real possibil-ity. Hoffmeyer writes, "The living world . . . can be awe inspiring or deeply moving and, whatever else it may be, it concerns us. It is made of the same stuff as we ourselves are—it resembles us because it dreamed us up."[18]

But to step back a moment, the end of both dualism and atom-ism came together in the work of Gregory Bateson. He started his long and eventful career as an anthropologist, and moved into nu-merous fields as he pursued his wide-ranging intellectual questions. Bateson's fundamental assertion is that the unit of survival is not the individual or the species, but is the organism-and-its-environment. It follows from this that an organism that deteriorates its environ-ment is committing suicide.[19] In his analysis, organism and environ-ment are influencing each other, co-evolving, becoming with each other through time. These propositions overthrow any sense of hyperseparation. Rather there is entanglement and interaction, a deep and abiding mutuality. This entangled quality of life on Earth depends on and supports connectivity. There are numerous ways into thinking about these matters. I offer one way: the kinship mode. It situates us here on Earth, and asserts that we are not alone in time or place: we are at home where our kind of life (Earth life) came into being, and we are members of entangled generations of Earth life, generations that succeed each other in time and place. In chapter 8, I return to these themes.

World making depends on uncertainty. The way of nature is the way of the new—the "creation of unpredictable novelty," as Prigogine puts it.[20] The unpredictability of nature's coming forth has created the complexity of life on Earth; complexity is endlessly interesting because it is never exhausted, and part of its interest for us is that it brought forth the creatures known as humans. We Westerners have named ourselves *Homo sapiens sapiens*—the thinking animal. The arrogance is evident, but it also contains a home truth: we are *a* species (certainly not *the* species) that wants to know. Our desire to know encounters the mystery inherent in the fact that knowing can never be complete, and we are hooked. Mystery and desire are terms that call to us in the language of sensuous experience, but they can also be defined technically. Mystery is an essential property of a holistic system. One cannot remove one's self from the system under examination, and because one is a part of the system one will always encounter mystery in the encounter with the integrity of larger systems. Desire, too, can be defined technically. It is the will toward self-realization that is characteristic of all life because life itself in all its many parts and processes is self-repairing, self-changing, and self-realizing. In humans, the desire for self-realization includes a desire for knowledge. Thus desire must always bring us into encounter with mystery, and mystery, properly understood (if that is not too paradoxical) would enhance our desire by being so close.

Margulis and Sagan define life as it works productively with time: life is always "preserving the past, making a difference between past and present; life binds time, expanding complexity and creating new problems for itself."[21] Life in this broader context is "a network of cross-kingdom alliances" that "help keep the entire planetary surface brimming with life."[22] As we lose the connectivities that make up the fabric of life on earth, we ourselves are less and less likely to be a sustainable species. Increasingly we seem to be one of the problems that life is confronting. Trotsky said it perfectly years and years ago in the context of war; in thinking expansively about his words we have to consider that war is not only an interhuman project but has expanded to become an interspecies project as well. You may not be interested in extinction, I would suggest in paraphrase, but extinction is interested in you.

The infatuation with certainty can be seen as a way to try to cut through the dynamics of mystery and desire; to distil clear boundaries and stability from dynamic fluctuation. Ecological existentialism enjoins us to live within the dynamics, and to pour our love into this unstable and uncertain Earth. Ethical questions within the world of connectivity start with how to appreciate the differences between humankind and others, while at the same time also understanding that we are all interdependent. How to engage in world making across species? How to work toward world making that enhances the lives of others? And how to do all this in the time of extinctions, knowing, as we must, that we are living amidst the ruination of others?

5. Orion's Dog

A good neighbour tells on and on, you know, that same rolling.—Edward Johnson, in "Transcript of Proceedings: North West Simpson Desert Land Claim (No. 126)"

I had a little breathing vent that was also my peephole. Tucked into my swag on a freezing night in the Simpson Desert of Central Australia, I could look out and watch the stars. Orion is one of the great night folk—in winter, in the desert, in the early hours when dark is all there is, Orion lies seductively low on the horizon. Even peering out through my little airhole, I could see him and feel happy.

He is said to be a mighty hunter, and maybe he is, but that's not what matters. Nobody who was just chasing rabbits would wear his belt slung low at that interesting and supremely attractive angle. He is chasing the Seven Sisters, and he really gives them a run—all over Australia, north and south, east and west, and all around the whole world. Call him what you will, everywhere people seem to know that it is women he's hunting. I knew him in North America, where I grew up with him, and when I came to Australia I started hearing about his adventures in this country. I imagined him wearing an Aboriginal belt—a well-ochred string with the brightest and shiniest of pearl shells strategically placed. Actually, I didn't fully appreciate the meaning of men's thighs until I saw Aboriginal men dance. Even the oldest greybeard can make you feel dizzy as you sit on the ground with your eyes fastened on . . .

. . . but these are not the best thoughts for a lady in a single swag on a night when it's way too cold even to go for a walk. Best to leave Orion to his nightly chase and try to get some sleep.

In the morning it was clear that the Seven Sisters had been running all around the camp that night. The tarp was covered with ice, and I could almost hear Uncle Fred Biggs telling the story. Roland Robinson wrote it up years ago and called it "The Star Tribes":

And there's those Seven Sisters, travelling
Across the sky. They make the real cold frost.
You hear them when you're camped out on the plains.
They look down from the sky and see our fire
And "Mai, mai, mai," they'd sing out as they run
Across the sky. And, when you wake, you find
Your swag, the camp, the plains, all white with frost.[1]

Such beauty, such stories, oh Lord what a morning!

The sky is full of stories wherever you go, but still I often felt lonely for the northern stars. When you say good-bye to your familiar night folk you feel a strange loss. Knowing that there are no bears here on the ground in Australia makes sense of the fact that there are no bears in the sky—they wouldn't fit. And yet, I like to think of them shining so beautifully in their own country.

It takes time to get to know new stars, but when I began to make their acquaintance I found that although I was far from the Bears, I was now close to Crocodiles—both to the sky folk and to their Earthly countrymen. At first I only knew of the Southern Cross through the words of Mark Twain. He was not impressed:

We are moving steadily southward—getting further and further down under the projecting paunch of the globe. Yesterday evening we saw the Big Dipper and the north star sink below the horizon and disappear from our world. . . . [But] My interest was all in the Southern Cross. I had never seen that. I had heard about it all my life, and it was but natural that I should be burning to see it. No other constellation makes so much talk. . . . Judging by the size of the talk which the Southern Cross had made, I supposed it would need a sky all to itself.

But that was a mistake. We saw the Cross to-night, and it is not large. Not large, and not strikingly bright. . . . It is ingeniously named, for it looks just as a cross would look if it looked like something else. . . .

It consists of four large stars and one little one. . . . One must ignore the little star, and leave it out of the combination—it confuses everything. If you leave it out, then you can make out of the four stars a sort of cross—out of true; or a sort of kite—out of true; or a sort of coffin—out of true.[2]

This was not much of an introduction to a group of stars whose stories I came to know and learned to cherish. My teachers in Yarralin and nearby communities know the Southern Cross as the Crocodile. What we see as stars are the men standing around him getting ready to spear him. What we see as darkness is the body of the croc. And the croc himself is the focus of a story that connects people, languages, cultures, trees, hunting, waterholes, trade routes, and the big winds of September. The story starts with the Owlet Nightjar Dreaming ancestor and his efforts to kill a big crocodile that was living in the main waterhole of the Nightjar's home country. His spears simply were not hard enough, so he had to go to a nearby country to get a special wood. He came home then and killed the croc, and after all that he decided to have a rest. While he was sleeping, some cheeky youngfellas came up and started cooking and eating his crocodile. When Old Man Nightjar woke up and realized what was going on, he called up a big wind that grabbed the boys and scattered them around the country.

People who belong to this country took me to see many of the parts of the story that are there today: the boys (now stones), Old Man's whiskers (also stones), and the waterhole. Other parts of the story have been destroyed. The tree that was sacred to Old Man Nightjar, for example, was bulldozed to make way for an airstrip.

The crocodile was thrown up into the sky and remains there today. When the Crocodile tilts in a certain way, it signals the part of the story when the winds come. And every year the winds do come.

How wonderful that in a world of flux and unpredictability, the travels of the stars also tell an Earth story—season by season, and year by year. And yet, in this time of escalating Earth deaths, the star stories may be suffering too. There is cold consolation in Brad Leithauser's poem "Zodiac: A Farewell." The poem's latter part reads:

The great ark of the zodiac
  Is adrift on an endless sea.
There's comfort in knowing its cargo can come
  To no harm from you and me,

That no storm of human contriving could
    Ever reach so far . . .
The constellations' great consolations
    Lie there: in how distant they are,
And how bright the way they, high and dry,
    Shelter in the open sky.[3]

Where Leithauser, like the ancient Greeks, finds consolation in distance, Indigenous stories describe lots of to-ing and fro-ing between Earth and Sky. Old Tim Yilngayarri's stories about Earth-Sky connections are especially precious to me because he was the only person in the region who had been there. He told how the Sky people had dropped a rope and taken him up to their country where they gave him special powers. And when he looked back at Earth he saw the fires of people's camps looking like stars. Old Tim left it open to us to imagine the reverse: that to look at stars is to see the campfires of the Sky country people. The old man has passed away, and perhaps there is a new distance as the lived connections are being lost. But surely closeness remains for as long as the stories are told and the songs are sung; surely, too, for as long as the Crocodile still shines, and the symmetries of wind and stars beat out their steady rhythm.

As I learned when I left the Northern Hemisphere, the Star folk are most fully alive when they are connected with their Earthly countrymen. Happily, dogs, like Orion, seem to be everywhere. In her exquisite essay "Oyez à Beaumont," Vicki Hearne reminds us of the moment in T. H. White's *The Sword in the Stone* when the great hound Beaumont, gored by a boar, lies dying. The huntsman kills him in compassion: he "let Beaumont out of this world, to run free with Orion and to roll among the stars."[4]

In Australia, the dogs are dingoes and they run with the Seven Sisters, not with Orion. Women and dogs! I can't help but feel happy about the protective mateship dogs offer us: how they chase guys who pester us, and bite the arms and legs of those who might harm us. Our old stories tell us this story too: that Artemis caused Actaeon to be transformed into a stag so that his own dogs would tear him to pieces because he had spied on her while she was bathing. Some Australian stories tell of how the crafty Sky hunter sent his penis underground to try to get to the Sisters, to ambush them from below, as it were. But the Sisters were not sitting on the ground, and they set their dingo mates on to him, urging them to savage the unwelcome visitor.[5] As Mark Twain would say, "let us draw the curtain of charity over the rest of the scene."[6]

Where the Seven Sisters go, dingo knowledge goes too. The Pleiades tell Old Tim's people that the dingo pups are being born, and when they make another shift they tell that the pups have opened their eyes. The old people, all those long gone generations of Aboriginal countrymen, would raid the dens, finding food and companions.

Today, though, dingoes are under sustained attack by pastoralists who mistakenly believe that the use of 1080 poison (sodium monofluoroacetate) will protect their vulnerable calves by diminishing the dingo population. In spite of scientific evidence, and in complete disregard of Indigenous people's views on the use of poison, the war against dingoes goes on. It is quite possible that the pastoralists will win. Like the Assyrians of old, many pastoralists descend on their dingo enemies with the bloodthirsty desire to annihilate them by death and dispersal. And like Tiglath-Pileser, who piled up the heads of defeated peoples "like heaps of grain,"[7] some pastoralists display their spoils of war, hanging the dead bodies of dingoes from trees, fences, and signposts.

If they win, if all the dens and families are dispersed, and even the lone survivors are hunted down or left to die of heartbreak, the only dingoes left will be in captivity. Like wolves and some domestic dogs, as well as many humans, they howl with grief and with lust, but one of their other primary motivations is to locate and communicate with other members of the group.[8] Their howling vocabulary is complex, and they sing out to their countrymen in harmonies that amplify the sound of their voices, telling each other who and where they are.[9]

I have often heard dingoes in the bush, and once I have actually been very, very close to a howling dingo. That was when I visited Dinky the Singing Dingo at Stuart Wells Roadhouse, south of Alice Springs. The owner of the roadhouse, Jim Cotterill, told me that Dinky's family was living in an area where 1080 was laid, and the nursing mother died. Some stockmen found her litter of six pups in a hollow under a sandhill. They put a trap outside, and it took about three days for the little pups to give up waiting for their mother and to come out. I do not understand why the stockmen took the pups back to the head station, since the purpose of 1080 was to kill them, but in any case, the owner knew that the Cotterills had a few animals at the pub. He rang and asked if they'd like a dingo. Jim said the pup was about six or eight weeks old when he got him. His pup-mates were all killed.

Jim's daughters play the piano, and when they practiced, Dinky started singing along with them. These days in the pub Dinky hops up on the piano and walks back and forth singing. According to Cotterill, "Every time someone starts playing the piano, Dinky creates a din. He starts howling, or singing as we call it. With a chair alongside the piano, he will walk up onto the keys—we call that his playing. He stands there and sings."[10] Dinky's singing is absolutely awesome, especially as he is willing to allow people to get very close. I taped him so that I could hear him whenever I wanted to. Only now I can't bear to listen. Not since I came to realize that I know this song; I have listened to it and sung it many times. From the Babylonian victory right up until today, the song cries out the anguish of exile and diaspora, of those who can never go home again. Part of the beauty of such songs is their improbability: that beauty should burst forth in the midst of disaster and despair seems miraculous. And the beauty is also the challenge and the heartbreak, expressing as it must the cruelty of those who, imagining transformation through destruction, seek the annihilation of others.

These are the days of violent extinctions, of global dimming and moving dust bowls, of habitat fragmentation, ice melt, and plundered lives. Animals are experiencing all this loss, and if we could better hear the waves of their agony, we would know this and be tormented. We would know that for the rest of our lives we will hear a growing chorus of increasingly diverse voices:

> For the wicked carried us away in captivity,
> > Required from us a song,
> How can we sing King Alfa's song in a strange land?[11]

I have heard the dingoes singing across the cliffs and gorges, across plains and deserts, and I cannot really comprehend that no matter how bright the night, or how sweet the air, there may come a day when we'll never hear them sing like that, ever. Not to their Sisters in the Sky country, or to the hunters in the Sky and on Earth, or for the love of their own kind, or in celebration of their own way of being in the world.

As yet another silence rolls out across the land, another wave of annihilation washes toward us, and again and again, there is the echo of the beautiful old African American spiritual:

My Lord
My Lord
Is this the morning
When the stars begin to fall?

6. Singing Up the Others

Eco-reconciliation: Living generously with the others, singing up relationships so that we all flourish.

Soulé's question about whether we will be able to love the others enough to want to save them is dire and urgent. We humans are Earth-born creatures. We evolved in the company of plants and animals, and the myriad other living things, all of us equally at home here on Earth. Inherent in each and every life is the fact that we are fragile creatures, dependent on resilient, but endlessly shifting, Earth systems. Whether we consider these matters deeply or superficially, theoretically or experientially, through action or statistics, nothing changes the fact that we are inexorably embedded in and sustained by webs of life and death.

The ecologist Paul Shepard holds that without our Earth companions, particularly animals, we cannot be human. He writes, "Our species . . . emerged in watching the Others, participating in their world by eating and being eaten by them, suffering them as parasites, wearing their feathers and skins, making tools of their bones and antlers, and communicating their significance by dancing, sculpting, performing, imaging, narrating, and thinking them."[1] Shepard's understanding of humanity's kinship with other living things is founded in evolution: in DNA and life's 4-billion-year history. Life has been diversifying itself into ever more life forms, and at the same time maintaining itself in its ancient forms. Evolutionary kinship gives us a "Möbius-strip quality of being": simultaneously we exist in two states, one of transformation away from others and one of kinship with them.[2]

When we think of relationships between ourselves and others as a matter of DNA, it is easy to imagine lineages, like branches of a tree. In this image, those who are closest to us are our near kin in time as well as in DNA. The tree image would put a DNA-distant species such as bacteria, for example, at a great temporal distance from our complex mammalian form of life. An alternative way of thinking about relationships is to consider the symbiosis which underlies the fact that we are all co-evolved here on Earth. This way of thinking reminds us that the bacterium which in one sense is an ancestor may at the same time and in this moment be living in our gut.[3] We are all participants in relationships that sustain us. Rather than branching lineages, symbiotic processes are better imagined as entangled connectivities, as interweaving paths and footprints, as waves of life and death.

Shepard's writings carry an ethical charge, calling us to understand and respect the kinship between ourselves and other animals. He challenges us to "discover how to cherish the world of life on its own terms."[4] From an ecologist's point of view, all living things are bound up in the webs of exchanges that make life possible. Aldo Leopold expressed this wonderfully in his essay "The Land Ethic," published posthumously in 1949. Recognizing that a fundamental question in ethics is the ability to discern between that which is good and that which is bad, he wrote, "A thing is right when it tends to preserve the integrity, stability and beauty of the biotic community. It is wrong when it tends otherwise."[5] His words give us a set of propositions about our species and its place in the world: that which is good contributes to the whole of a living system; we are part of that system; we are interdependent with other parts of that system.

Lynn Margulis and Dorion Sagan's book *What Is Life?* is a delightful exploration of the biology of life on Earth. Each chapter offers a definition of life that captures and expands the definition of the preceding chapter. Margulis and Sagan state that life's aim is to "preserve vivified matter in the face of adversity and a universal tendency toward disorder."[6] A key term in this literature is "autopoiesis," developed by the ecologists Humberto Maturana and Francisco Varela. Autopoiesis depends on processes of self-organization and self-repair.[7] Organic beings from single cells to the whole biosphere proactively seek life. Autopoiesis refers to life's continuous production of itself.[8] An important criticism of the autopoiesis theory is mounted by Donna Haraway. I am not able to judge the science involved, yet I remain persuaded by the idea that each of us is both differentiated and connected, and thus that autonomy and connectivity together constitute a dance of life. The essence of autopoiesis is the process of changing to stay the same: in a world of flux the capacity to stay (more or less) the same is accomplished through change.[9] Life's desire for life requires change and flux. Margulis and Sagan state that "mind and body, perceiving and living, are equally self-referring, self-reflexive processes already present in the earliest bacteria. Mind, as well as body, stems from autopoiesis."[10]

Death is completely central to life for us and many other beings. The exception is that some bacteria can survive more or less forever as copies are made again and again through cell division. In contrast, "programmed death," in which cells age and die as part of the life of the individual, came into the world with reproduction.[11] The link between desire (Eros) and death (Thanatos) is apparently coded into our DNA. Organisms die, but new non-copy organisms are brought into being.[12] Life, therefore, is an extension of itself into new generations and new species.[13] From an ecological point of view, death is a return. The body returns to bacteria, and bacteria return the body to the living earth.[14]

Our interdependence is our blessing and our strength. But as we are increasingly beginning to understand because it is all falling apart, our interdependence is also a source of peril. Collectively we humans have never lived in an era remotely like the one we are now entering. We are learning how to talk about the massive shifts called "climate change," the overwhelming losses taking place with accelerating rates of extinction, and the sudden instability of systems that for so long seemed to be stable. We can speak abstractly, but the issues are immediate and urgent. In a few short centuries, the human species has begun unmaking the balance on earth between life and death, enabling death to expand and expand, tilting life toward a catastrophe that is difficult to imagine, difficult to think, and yet morally imperative to consider. Along with the loss of existing life forms, there is a further, equally critical, loss of new life forms. This means that in our day species being lost are not being replaced.[15] We are seeing the death of evolution in many large classes of life forms. We do not know, and perhaps cannot know, how to think catastrophe on so large a scale. Western philosophy is limited because the catastrophe concerns animals and plants, life forms that for long had been held to be outside the bounds of ethical consideration.

Aboriginal people in Australia talk about "singing up the country." Their actions are designed to give life a charge, a boost, a call of care and connection. Singing up is relational; it communicates the fact that people are participating in the webs of life. This is a two-way process. In singing up others, people sing up themselves, their love, their knowledge, their way of fitting into country. Singing up is always specific. People sing up their own country, their animal and plant relations, their water and rain, their stories. Singing up opens the life of country, exposing the participatory quality of world making. However, Aboriginal people are not singing up the whole Earth. Rather, they are singing up the life-in-country which is the life that brought them forth and for which they are responsible. Singing up expresses powerful connectivities founded in knowledge, recognition, care, and love.

The Australian philosopher Freya Mathews has borrowed the term "singing up" and links it to the idea that Western peoples are in need of places where the dramas of encounter and recognition between humans and other living beings, and between humans and flourishing ecosystems, can occur. Singing up is work that fosters encounter and promotes flourishing relationships. In singing up the country, or singing up the others, one is singing one's self into the world of life, and singing the world of life into greater complexity. Thus, to sing up is to engage ethically and joyfully with the living world, to face the others with caring intention.[16]

The opposite of singing up is the death work that causes expanding fields of emptiness. Whether planned or accidental, extinctions result from actions that refuse to recognize connectivity, mutuality, and the flourishing of beings and relationships. The controversies surrounding the future of the Australian dingo offer an extreme case within which to consider the contrasts between singing up and wiping out.

The species *Canis lupus dingo* is a relative newcomer in Australia, having arrived about five thousand years ago from Southeast Asia. Dingoes rapidly acclimatized to the continent, spreading out across all the major ecological zones from tropical rainforests and savannas, to deserts, to freezing alpine regions. Aboriginal people learned the life cycle; they knew when the dingoes would be whelping, and when the pups would open their eyes. People would go out and raid a few dens, eating some of the pups and bringing a few back to camp as pets. Some dingoes became food, some became pets, many remained at home in the bush, and they all lived together like this for millennia.[17]

Dingoes provided a companionship that had never before existed in Australia. These creatures were the first nonhumans who answered back, came when called, helped in the hunt, slept with people, and learned to understand some of the vocabulary of human languages. As Adam O'Neill, a great respecter of dingoes, writes, "Unlike any other animal, the dog possesses a universal language understood by all people. We have a mutual understanding of the language of dogs, a language of tone, pitch, expression and gesture."[18] People gave them names, fitted them into the wider kinship structure, and took care of dead dingoes in the same way they took care of dead people. Dingoes have been fitted into the sacred geography as extremely powerful Dreamings, and they now figure prominently in ritual, songlines, and stories.

As I try to imagine the first encounters between Aboriginal people and dingoes, I see dingoes making the first moves toward companionship. They knew more about interacting with people than these people knew about dogs. The companionship appears to have developed rapidly. Aboriginal people were doing what humans have done for thousands of years, as archaeological and written records demonstrate: they were forming close, loving bonds of mutual care and solidarity with uniquely interactive companions.

For their part, dingoes had a lot of ecological learning to do. They found themselves in the driest inhabited continent on Earth, and they would have had to learn (if they did not already know) what every successful predator has to learn: to live in a balanced relationship with their food. The learning was perhaps uniquely demanding in Australia. The boom-and-bust cycles of the Australian climate and the relatively low fertility of much of the continent mean that successful species are those that are able to limit their numbers. Dingo families have very low reproductive rates. Unlike domestic dogs, female dingoes breed only once a year, and unless there is reason to increase the population (for example, in response to a drastic drop), only one litter of pups is raised within the family group even if there are several females. Living in extended family groups, young dingoes learn the territory, the behavior of prey, how to hunt cooperatively to bring down large animals such as kangaroos, and how to fit into the family structure. Marj Oakman, secretary of the Dingo Conservation Association, puts it this way: it takes a mother and a father to raise a dingo.

The complexity of human-dingo relationships emerges from both sides of the relationship. Dingoes are both "wild" and able to become domestic pets, although dingo experts caution that a pet dingo is nothing like an ordinary pet dog. On the human side, Aboriginal people love dingoes in their way, and many Euro-Australian people love dingoes in their way. Conservation biologists are learning more and more about the key role of dingoes in sustaining indigenous biodiversity and are active in trying to protect dingoes both for their own sake and for the sake of their ecological benefit. At the same time, there are Euro-Australians who loathe dingoes unyieldingly, considering them to be vermin. Some Aboriginal people are situated ambivalently between love and loathing. Some people keep them as pets; others make their living by killing them. For many people, the dingo is an iconic animal, its beauty and exceptionalism a key figure in a wider aesthetic of Australia's own beauty and exceptionalism.

The dominant Euro-Australian attitude toward dingoes will be familiar to everyone who has considered European people's long hatred of wolves, described so eloquently in Barry Lopez's book *Of Wolves and Men*.[19] As with wolves in the United States, in Australia the new settlers' effort to eradicate dingoes was based on the view that dingoes were detrimental to sheep and cattle, and therefore would not be tolerated. Graziers refer to rogue dogs who kill or maim hundreds of sheep in a single night, to dogs that gang up and threaten people who are out walking the country, to the cruelty of the dogs, and to the negligence of national parks personnel and policy. Some of their accounts are ridiculously overstated, but most express concern for the well-being of their flocks and for their own livelihoods.[20] The desire to protect their livelihood results in the desire among many (not all) graziers to eradicate forever the animal they call their enemy.

In contrast, Old Tim and other Dingo people were completely

against efforts to eradicate or "control" dingoes. Tim was the only person in our area who understood dog language, and for that reason he was something of a spokesman. I asked Old Tim what dogs said to him, and he told me (among other things), "'We don't come bash up people,' they say. 'What for people want to bash up us?'" Tim's commentary was clear: "Anyone who reckons dogs are too dirty to lick my pannikin, and hit them and hit them, no good. We come out of that dog. No good hit them, no good shoot them. Dog's a big boss, you've gotta leave him be, no more killing." In his stories, the ancestral Dingoes give voice to their sense of lost reciprocity, and to current grievance: "I made them man and woman. Now you've dropped me, put me in the rubbish dump."[21]

The killing has been relentless. Prior to 1947, dingo-proof fences were erected and maintained by pastoralists with the idea of keeping dingoes out of areas where local populations had been annihilated. Starting in 1947, state governments decided to rationalize and systematize a fence which is now some 3,290 miles (5,400 kilometers) long.[22] According to James Woodford, who has traveled the fence, it "is an ecological Berlin Wall comparable to the Great Wall of China."[23]

THIS GATE SHOULD BE CLOSED
AT ALL TIMES
IF FOUND OPEN PLEASE CLOSE

Warri Gate, part of the Dingo Fence, New South Wales/Queensland border.
(AUTHOR'S PHOTO)

The fence is meant to control the movement of animals. In itself it does not eradicate them. In areas of western New South Wales, where a country road goes through the fence there is a large gate. You have to stop and open the gate in order to drive through; you can't miss seeing the signs that advise in no uncertain terms that fines apply if gates are left open, and that this is all being managed by the "Wild Dog Destruction Board."

The fence has had disastrous effects on other animals as well as dingoes. Woodford reports numerous instances of animals dying along the fence because they were unable to get through. Perhaps the most devastating recent report comes from January 2001, when high temperatures forced animals to travel widely in search of water. He writes, "Nothing could have prepared me for the sight of 1000 [camel] corpses and at least as many kangaroo and emu remains."[24] He continues: "The one person who gained the most from the mass death on the fence was an old Croatian dogger, Ted Grabovack. He severed hundreds of camel humps, laced them with strychnine and hung them on the fence to poison dingoes." This dogger liked to "show off about the numbers of dingoes he had shot and trapped," and he displayed the bodies by stringing them up on the fence wire.[25] This custom is still practiced; not only by doggers, but by graziers and other rural workers who hang dingo corpses from gates, trees and signposts, or throw them across fences.

Along with fences, there are traps, poisons, and bullets. Traps are controversial because of the cruelty involved, and are illegal in some places. Poison and shooting are both widespread today. Poison is controversial for its side effects. Strychnine lingers in the corpse, so animals that scavenge are also likely to be killed. The poison 1080 has similar effects; it has been said to be safer than strychnine but evidence suggests otherwise.[26] Not only is 1080 widely used against dingoes, but it is also used in some areas by farmers and foresters to protect crops and trees from native animals such as possums, quolls, and wallabies.[27] Formerly (and continuing today in some areas) there was a bounty on dingoes; shooters scalped the animals and tendered the scalps for payment. In some years, dingo scalping was a way for many people, Aboriginal and Settler Australian, to make a living; according to Woodford, in the period 1920–34, bounties were paid on five hundred thousand scalps in South Australia.

In the longer term, scalping proved ineffective. Scalpers, or doggers, do not have an interest in eradicating the species from which they gain their livelihood, and it is to be expected that they will not attempt total eradication. According to one expert, "scalp bonuses do not control predators and are a waste of money."[28] In addition to the effects of poison and shooting, recent studies also indicate that land clearing is responsible for turning dingoes toward sheep and calves. As their habitat is destroyed, their territories are broken up and their regular prey are eradicated.

Research into the role of the dingo as a participating member of Australian ecosystems is still very new, and has been stimulated by the work of Soulé and other conservation biologists who have been developing analysis of the role of top predators in sustaining ecosystems—wolves in Yellowstone National Park, dingoes in Australia, among others. There is now good evidence that where dingo populations are intact, they work to sustain a balance of species that is viable in the long term. There is a strong correlation between healthy dingo populations and biodiversity as indicated by the flourishing presence of native species.

The Australian case is instructive. Australia has the highest rate of mammalian extinctions in the world today. Recent studies indicate that persecution of dingoes is a major factor.[29] What does a predator do in a flourishing ecosystem? A major cause of extinction, along with habitat loss, is the introduction of foxes and cats, both of which have gone bush and thrived magnificently on the small marsupials who previously had no experience of being hunted so intensely. Cats and foxes do not limit their population the way dingoes do, and as a consequence their numbers grow out of proportion to their resource base. If it were not for the rabbits, another introduced species of European origin, the foxes and cats might have driven even more native species extinct, but by the same token, rabbit plagues enabled foxes and cats to sustain very high numbers.

The role of the dingo is crucial in controlling foxes and cats. Predator competition is at work here, and dingoes allow very few other predators into their territories. At the same time, dingoes have far less impact on native species compared to introduced predators, at least when they thrive in family and territorial groups. As a consequence, where dingoes are present and healthy, biodiversity

Bush Dingo in outback Queensland.
(PHOTO COURTESY OF JOHN MURRAY)

is greater. In areas where dingoes are eradicated, or where their territorial control is disrupted, foxes and cats flourish. Recently, therefore, conservationists who are working to sustain the biodiversity of
native species have been arguing for the necessity of healthy dingo
families.[30] Adam O'Neill draws on a lifetime of experience with dingoes and other predators (cats and foxes in particular) to make an
extremely forceful statement: "I believe that the dingo is our only
chance for eco-reconciliation."[31]

A recently completed study by Arian Wallach and Adam O'Neill
offers very strong conclusions: loss of dingoes means loss of species
richness. Dingoes increase small mammal abundance and diversity;
through ecological cascades dingoes increase vegetation abundance.
Most importantly, perhaps: "threatened species survive in the wild
only under the protective influence of dingoes."[32]

Ongoing efforts to kill dingoes or destroy their habitat often have
the paradoxical effect of exacerbating the problem. O'Neill explains
that because dingoes are highly socialized animals, the killing breaks
up stable family groups, and destroys the local culture. "Their social
organisation and territorial ties to land are lost," O'Neill explains.[33]
Young, relatively unsocialized animals move into territory that has
been vacated, and they are naïve to the dangers associated with humans.[34] The dingo in the photo was encountered in outback Queensland and is so young and naïve as to be almost heartbreaking. It

showed no fear, and was lucky the human carried a camera rather than a gun.

Under pressure of eradication efforts, dingoes breed prolifically, and if they have not learned to hunt together, they go for the relatively defenseless sheep and calves. In O'Neill's terms, man's use of poison forces dingoes "to live in a perpetual state of social disorder."[35] Starving, dysfunctional, out of control, they turn to domestic animals.[36]

To gaze into the eyes of a wild animal is to look into mystery. Perhaps the gaze is so awesome because we know that we have almost no idea how the animal sees us. We look across this chasm and see eyes that are much like our own. We see the intelligence that gleams there, and often it is baffling as well as beautiful.

Dingoes may be an exception. David Jenkins is a Canberra-based scientist who has spent years working with dingoes in the bush. Recently he was asked whether he felt afraid when he was with or near dingoes. Jenkins says the animals tend to be curious rather than aggressive. "I've never felt in any sort of danger. But when these animals look at you, they look really hard. There's something really going on in that hard-wired brain. It's not the same feeling as when a Labrador looks at you."[37] Perhaps dingoes know a predator species when they see one. When they look at a human, they want to know what that predator is going to do. They are seeing their brothers and sisters, perhaps, and it may be that they know us better than we know ourselves.

The war against dingoes takes us into the shadow of death, where extinction is a near possibility. Dingo deaths are one ripple in the larger pattern of destruction that calls us to ask: Is eco-reconciliation nothing more than a wild and crazy dream? Is it necessary that all animals become either pets or enemies? Is there no room for the companionability of others who share with us the glories of life without being directly beholden to us in any particular way?

These are good questions, and there are more. They go to Bobby, and the exclusion of animals from human ethics, and to our growing awareness that actually we are all part of a kindred of life on Earth. Lopez's beautiful words articulated in relation to wolves can be said in relation to dingoes, and other top predators. Increasingly, they can be said in relation to a great number of animals and plants whose lives are disappearing under a variety of human pressures: "In the end, I think we are going to have to go back and look at the stories we made up when we had no reason to kill, and find some way to look the animal in the face again."[38]

7. Job's Grief

An animal caught in the bright lights of the shooters does not run. It is stunned into stillness just at that moment before death guns it down. Suddenly there is a reverberating loneliness—no one wants to be inside that bright and deathful space, and there is a shattering silence. In this harsh light we see for a moment just how quickly and callously death can be blasted into our world, how it can torture before killing, by isolating and silencing, how it constructs a space in which a living being is suspended briefly between the world of joyful life and the long tumble into the abyss.

The biblical book of Job gives us a vivid account of the poetics of this space between life and death.[1] More than any other thinker today, the Australian biblical scholar Norman Habel presses us to consider how God has spotlighted Job.[2] As long as Job was held in God's scrutiny, he could not escape; God would not allow him to die, nor would he allow Job to live as a whole human being. God isolated Job several times over, singling him out for disaster. When Satan offered the wager—that Job would no longer love God if God should ruin everything else that Job loved—God crushed Job. Then God withheld himself, denying dialogue. Furthermore, God denied Job any human comfort. This man who sought to overcome God's silence, to press God into answering him, is both our kinsman and our death mate. His story impels us into a domain of anguish, and often there seems to be no way out.

I want to circle away from Job, leaving him spotlighted in the ruins of his life, but promising to return once we have explored a resonating story from Aboriginal Australia.

In Yarralin, I also listened to stories of wager and willful death; the stories there involved the Moon and the Dingo. As I heard Old Tim, Daly Pulkara, and other Dingo Lawmen tell the stories of the space between life and death, the Moon was offering eternal life to the Dingo. The stories are not meant to be 100 percent clear as parts are held within a domain of secrecy. In summary, the Moon's claim to fame is that he dies and returns as himself. Every month he disappears, and every month he comes back. There is no death for the Moon. There is, however, a terrible loneliness. He has no mates, no fellow creatures; there is only the one Moon. So he offers Dingo eternal life, but there is a catch. The Dingo will have to become a sycophant of the Moon. The Dingo refuses, and so the Moon starts taunting him and daring him, urging him to die and return, to try to do as the Moon does.

"Die," the Moon said. "Die as I do and come back again in four days' time." The Dingo reckoned he couldn't do it. But the Moon kept daring him, and so he decided to take the gamble. As Daly told the story, the Dingo knew it wouldn't work, and his final words were, "You can't see me come out in four days. I'll go forever." And that is what happened.

Unlike the Moon, the Dingo was not alone. His mates were there too, and they called out to him, "What's the good, poor bugger? Come back, come back . . ." Again and again they called, but he was truly gone. People are related to dingoes, and as dingoes die, so we die. Quoting Daly again, "We follow that dog. We never did it differently." Sometimes he added, "Look like we made a little bit of a mistake there!"

So there he was, this Dreaming Dingo, pressured into a contest he thought he would lose, and then abandoned by the Moon who had persuaded him. Daly and others heaped blame on the Moon: "Why that Moon never go back and help him?" Daly asked, clearly putting the case that the Moon should have had some feeling for the Dingo and helped him come back. "That Moon should have said: 'Ah, that's bad. No good you stay dead like that. Why don't you come back again?'"

The Moon's triumph was a total win, but at the cost of connection with others. He goes away and returns, always himself, over and over again, never dying, but never sharing his life with others. His triumph is equally his loneliness, for he has no relationship with the world and all its contingent and glorious living things with all their passions, their desires, their songs, and their deaths.

What did the Dreaming Dingo think? I wonder, as he struggled against the finality of death. He may have heard the Moon laughing in triumph, and I imagine he poured forth a great howling lamentation as he disappeared forever. But at the same time he would have heard his mates. Their voices, raised in the haunting harmonies of dingoes, kept calling "Come back, come back . . ." Their penetrating songs would have accompanied him into his death, their voices mingling with his and holding the songs of grief aloud in the world even as their mate died. These beautiful wailing voices offered solidarity in the moment of death, and they sang into the face of the Moon who was so coldly triumphal and so terribly isolated.

Similarly, but not identically, there was Job, betrayed, abandoned, isolated by God. He calls out to God, and for a long time there is no answer. *"I cry out to You, but You do not answer me; / I wait, but You do not consider me."*[3] When I think of Job and the Dingo as two creatures who shared a similar experience, the contrast heightens Job's loneliness. The first abandonment was the wager, in which God decided to experiment with him, destroying his fields and flocks and killing all his children. The second abandonment was the isolation. Who called to him in his sorrow, who offered comfort, who was there for him? His wife encouraged him in his longing for death, and his three self-righteous friends lost all empathy or compassion. The friends were proponents of certainty, and they wanted to sustain their sense of the certainty of God by trying to justify Job's suffering. To this end they kept telling him that he must deserve it. Job, often called the first great existentialist, refused to submit to their arguments.[4] His wife told him to curse God and die, and he did not die, nor did he curse God. Even as he called on God to break through his silence, he was tormented by hooligans.

> *Time and again you humiliate me,*
> *And are not ashamed to abuse me*
>
> . . . .
>
> *All my bosom friends detest me;*
> *Those I love have turned against me.*[5]

Let us listen to Job's words as a call for connection—that God not isolate him, and that the world not abandon him in his sorrow. As far as the story tells us, his cries fell into emptiness. The spotlight was on him, and he was alone.

W. G. Sebald was one of the greatest twentieth-century essayists on destruction and death space. In his exquisite piece "Campo Santo," he leads the reader into a devastating contemplation of the loneliness of death arising out of the condition of life in our time, a time when "everyone is instantly replaceable and is really superfluous."[6] I read Sebald and become almost breathless with the slowly accumulating complexity and power of his deceptively straightforward writing. This is another form of loneliness, not pain, Sebald says, but rather a great forgetting: "Now that we have reached a point where the number of those alive on earth has doubled within just three decades and will treble within the next generation . . . the significance of the dead is visibly decreasing." In the end, he suggests, "we shall ourselves relinquish life without feeling any need to linger at least for a while."[7]

Reflecting on these two kinds of loneliness, one of abandonment, the other of superfluity, my thoughts shift toward Aboriginal ways of managing dying. As I noted, when a person was near death, Old Tim would go after their spirit, calling them to come back. He would return with a report then, either bringing the spirit back to the body for a time, or telling all the crying relations that the person really was going into death.

With each death and each funeral people cried out in anguish, drawing others into the region of death and dying so that no one in that torn space was isolated or silenced. Through all the anger, the negotiation and conflict, and all the invocations of loss and love conveyed through song and tears and calls of sorrow, funerals reached out to the individuality of the dead person, to their country, and to the spirits that may have been walking about, to the Dreamings that take notice, to the family, to the custodians of the dead, and to the stories, like the Dingo and Moon. All this grieving reaches out into the death space, and if life is truly finished, then all this grieving sought a response from the living, sought voices that howl in sympathy and assure us all that neither the living nor the dying have been abandoned. This was a sharing of grief so as to soothe the throbbing emptiness left in the country, and in the family, and in the world more widely. Shared grief brought death into the world of life.

The worst funeral I ever experienced shone a spotlight on the loneliness that arises when the sharing of grief breaks down. Some Pentecostal missionaries had brought into our region a way of thinking about death that was not only foreign but, I think, inhuman. The idea was that we should rejoice because our brother or sister had gone to heaven, that better world, that home on high, where they could finally join Jesus and live in eternal bliss. There were many terrible funerals. The worst one became chaotic because the missionaries and their followers were running one kind of funeral, and the rest of the people, the unconverted folk, were running another kind of funeral—all at the same time. So when Mollie, the oldest wife of the dead man, threw herself violently onto the ground crying and sobbing, there was no one there to cushion her or hold her. And when people started to bang their heads, where were the relations who would restrain them? I shall never forget Mollie's look when she realized that her grief was not being responded to. Abandoned in that moment, like Job in his misery, she was suddenly naked in the shock of realization that her world had just fallen to pieces—not only because her husband of a lifetime had died, but now, again, and even more shatteringly, because her grief found no response. The lamentation that should have called forth harmonies fell into an unfathomable silence.

I was beside myself with anguish both for Mollie and for her husband, a man I respected enormously. This cacophonous event set us all on edge, and we who should have been helping him through death were stumbling and mishandling everything. The thought of his spirit trying to find its way back to country with no harmonies to carry it along was awful. My consolation was in feeling certain this terrible event was not the final story. Once the missionaries were gone and their funeral was over, the real work of singing him home could begin.

Stories of the Moon and the Dingo also tell the story of what happens after death. Yes, death is final in the sense that the persons or dingoes never return as themselves, but at the same time, various spirits continue to live, and some will return in other bodies, other lives, other families, perhaps even other countries. Old Tim told the story: "That kid finds a new father, new mother: that's the Dingo

Law. . . . The dead man looks around, thinks about his Dreaming. . . . Makes himself into kangaroo, goanna, bird, crocodile. . . . That's the Law. From that Dog."

One's life will indeed be extinguished, but life itself is a process of ongoing cross-species transformations, and as participants in that process, human beings share in its continuity. Part of the importance of singing the person into death and then on into their home country is to ensure that death is not so final, that people or dogs remain where they belong, and that death is turned back toward life even though the individual will never, like the Moon, experience the selfsame life. Those beautiful songs, those howling harmonies, sing the dying person through death and into the great turning.

Job's situation was different. Stephen Mitchell expresses Job's dilemma perfectly in his translation:

> Like a cloud fading in the sky,
>   man dissolves into death.
> He leaves the world behind him
>   and never comes home again.[8]

Habel's insightful Earth reading finds Job longing to rest at peace within the Earth. Sheol, in Habel's interpretation, is not a lonely shadow land, but rather a place where people are securely sheltered from the capricious cruelty of Heaven.[9]

Job's longing for return to Earth can also be imagined in the context of ancestor veneration. The archaeologist and historian Rachel Hallote demonstrates through her extensive research that the Bible disguises how people in that era perceived death. "Most Israelites worshipped their dead family members by feeding them and praying to them," she writes.[10] Dead people were considered still to be part of the family. They were buried in caves, or under the house, or in the fields, and connections between the dead and living were kept alive through acts of veneration that included sharing food, and consulting the dead about the future. Those who were dying expected their surviving relations to put their body to rest with their ancestors, so that they could join their people in their place, and remain in connection with their descendants.

Such veneration of the dead depends on the family, perhaps most vividly embodied in the wider group known as the "house." In the ancient world the house, in addition to being a space and a place, was also a set of relationships that people sought to sustain across generations by binding their children into the future of the house, bringing in wives for the sons and husbands for the daughters.[11] The house of Job had been thriving, and it was this whole house that God wiped out when he killed all the sons and daughters, and all the flocks and crops that would have provided for them.

God abandoned Job severely then, because with no descendants there would be no living people to hold open his connection with the living world. Once dead he would be dead twice over—first having lost his place as a living member of the world of life, and then losing the possibilities of connections with the living world after his death. He was looking into his own extinction. It may be that his longing to be returned back into the womb of Earth, as Habel explains, is also a recognition of the fact that with everything destroyed, the finality of Earth was now his last and sweetest hope for rest.

Where, then, is my hope?
Who can see hope for me?
Will it descend to Sheol?
Shall we go down together to the dust?[12]

When God destroyed the house, he stole Job's afterlife as well as his current life. Truly, Job was isolated. There would be no one left to wail over him, no one to sing him into his grave, no future for him once his body died. God did what the Moon did not manage to do to the Dingo—he ruined Job's death just as surely as he ruined his life.

So there was Job, isolated and alone on his pile of ashes, scraping away at his suppurating flesh; we understand why people shunned him. And yet, Habel's Earth reading shows us that Job did have company of a sort. The book of Job asserts that the oppressive force of God's "hand is experienced by all life—animals, birds, fish and Earth itself. . . . Job does not suffer alone."[13]

Job claims a kinship of suffering with the wider Earth, but perhaps there was also a more intimate connection. I imagine that when all Job's animals were killed, his house dogs as well as his herd dogs died. But then, as now, there were stray dogs roaming the streets and back alleys, some of them abandoned, some simply adventurous. What if one of them found Job and settled in beside him, sharing his food and the warmth of his campfire? Being a dog, she would not be fussy about open sores and flaking skin, bad breath or loathsome odors. More than that, she would see him not as a sickly shell but as a full human. Looking into his eyes would she see that in spite of all the rejection by God and by man, there was still the desire for connection that he had kept alive within the loneliness of his grief? The Dingo who was taunted by the Moon had his Dingo mates. Why should Job not have a dog?

Let us call her Blackie in honor of the dark-colored guard dogs of the ancient world; she is, surely, kin to the dogs of Egypt during the Exodus.[14] She would lick Job's hands, wagging her tail, and gazing at him in quick, doglike devotion. Her gift was that she was not afraid of the deathful spotlight. Her ancestors had been here before her, and they had learned the truth of this place. They knew they would have to die, and they knew how to sing to their mates, calling them back, or carrying them through to more life. In this space of wager and death, they sang the connections that cross the abyss. Even if no one else was left to grieve for Job, and even though God seemed indifferent, Blackie would howl over his dead body and sing him into Earth.

So when God finally did appear with his whirlwind and his seemingly endless elaboration of his power, Job was not alone. Blackie, too, listened to God's voice as it emerged from the whirlwind, and she too heard echoes of the triumphalist Moon as God extolled the enormity of his power:

> Where were you when I planned the earth?
>   Tell me, if you are wise.
> Do you know who took its dimensions,
>   measuring its length with a cord?
> What were its pillars built on?
>   Who laid down its cornerstone,
> while the morning stars burst into singing
>   and the angels shouted for joy![15]

God spoke like this for a long time. Blackie rested her head on Job's legs, and he draped his arm across her neck. They listened together, and their mateship enabled Job to understand something new. When Job acknowledged God's greatness, saying dryly, "I know, you can do everything,"[16] he may have been heaping blame on God in the way that Daly and others heaped blame on the Moon. At the same time, he was pointing out that there were things God could not do. He was suggesting that God could not find a mate who would lick his hands and sing him home. That awareness was possible because of Blackie. She gave him an understanding of God's limits, and so Job was moved to recognize that God was so powerful that he had no true others. Like the Moon, without others he lacked the capacity for dramas of encounter, recognition, and compassion. He would always win, but the price was utter loneliness.

Job might have thought back to the Garden of Eden, to Adam and Eve, and he might have thought that when they ate the forbidden fruit and became like gods a terrible loneliness descended upon them. God's curse was then a doubled curse; that they would die (unlike God) and that they would lose their understanding of, and capacity for being part of, Earth life. They would not know how to fit, and would only know how to dominate. Thinking themselves to be all-powerful, like gods, their awareness of the underlying Earth kinship, the mateship of all those born to die, would be obscured for them. Lost in the deepest possible sense, they would venture alone down ever more ghastly paths of utility, cruelty, and alienation.

The Bible story tells us that Job repented. I wonder if he was using God's language of power in order to communicate to God that he gave up his desire for knowledge because the one thing about which he was certain was that he did not want to be, or be like, God. Was Job able to see that to face death one needs mates, that the blessing of Earth-life is the comfort of others? Dog and human, as the Aboriginal stories tell us, know that the death space calls for mates, Earth mates, who will enter into terror and reach out to each other, and who will call out in all seriousness and with all willful intention: "Come back, come back."

Now, in this era of extinctions, we are in the midst of both kinds of loneliness. Animals and plants, all our precious Earth mates, are abandoned as they tumble into deaths that have no return. Their future generations are eradicated, and their deaths are treated as if they were superfluous. Who sings out to them? Or do their calls fall into a lonely death space where the powerful, enchanted with their own success and indifferent to disaster, turn away from the faces of others?

Along with the activism required of us in these days of grief, let us not forget to keep singing:

Come back, you gods of old Earth ~
   Sun bear, Moon bear, Panda, Polar, Grizzly
Come back, you desert dwellers ~
   Bilby, Potoroo, Nail tail, Bandicoot
Come back, you majestic singers ~
   Texas Gray, Japanese, Southern Rocky, Timberwolf
Come back, dear mates ~
   Dear Jackal, Wild dog, Dingo.

As loneliness descends, and the spotlight grows larger ~
   Come back,
   Or take us with you,
   But leave us not alone without you, forever,

Come back ~

8. What If the Angel of History Were a Dog?

W alter Benjamin, literary critic, translator, essayist, and philosopher, died by his own hand when he was trying to escape from Nazi Germany and, blocked at the border, couldn't face being sent back. His essays have an impact that keeps growing in the aftermath of his death, perhaps in part because they are snatched from the Holocaust and speak so directly to the catastrophe of civilization. One of the most influential short pieces is his ninth thesis on the philosophy of history. It begins with a stanza of poetry by Gerhard Scholem followed by a text that reads:

> A Klee painting named "Angelus Novus" shows an angel looking
> as though he is about to move away from something he is fixedly
> contemplating. His eyes are staring, his mouth is open, his wings
> are spread. This is how one pictures the angel of history. His face
> is turned toward the past. Where we perceive a chain of events,
> he sees one single catastrophe which keeps piling wreckage upon
> wreckage and hurls it in front of his feet. The angel would like to
> stay, awaken the dead, and make whole what has been smashed.
> But a storm is blowing from Paradise; it has got caught in his wings
> with such violence that the angel can no longer close them. This
> storm irresistibly propels him into the future, to which his back is
> turned, while the pile of debris before him grows skyward. This
> storm is what we call progress.[1]

This is one of the great texts of the twentieth century, and the fact that it speaks so directly to us today suggests that it holds its value in this century as well. Every sentence offers ideas for engagement, but for me the most compelling segment concerns the wreckage that is catastrophe. All living things are caught up in the wreckage of our time. Let us consider some of the implications of the howling of living beings in this time of escalating death.

There are two big contexts of death. The first is the fact that death resides within life. With the exception of some bacteria, life involves death both for individuals and, in much longer time frames, for most species. Death, as a corollary to life, happens to all of us complex creatures. It may happen through old age, or illness; it may happen through hunting or killing; it may happen on larger scales through events such as cyclones, earthquakes, or volcanoes. In this context, living things are bound into ecological communities of life and death, and within these communities life is always making and unmaking itself in time and place.

The second context differs from the first in being a uniquely human invention: man-made mass death.[2] This form of death arises out of a will-to-destruction that seems to be confined to humans. Contemporary scholars' interest in this phenomenon arises most vigorously out of the death world of the Holocaust, but the term is appropriate to all instances of genocide. The will-to-destruction can most vividly be thought of as death work. It involves imagining a future emptiness, and then working systematically to accomplish that emptiness. Scholars working in this field contend that the will-to-destruction defiles both life and death. In ordinary life, death is the necessary completion of life. Man-made mass death is not necessary and does not complete life. Instead it is a massive interruption, a negation of the relationships between life and death. If we contemplate such death work from the standpoint of animals, we can expand the idea to include anthropogenic extinctions. The analysis of genocide can become an analysis of biocide. But first let us revisit questions of "certainty" and suffering.

Innocent Suffering

"Theodicy" is the technical term for intellectual efforts to understand why suffering exists. It is hard to imagine that there are humans anywhere on Earth who do not wonder about this, but it is a preoccupation of Western religion and philosophy because of the logical theorizing about God. If, as is claimed in Christianity, God is all-knowing, all-seeing, and wholly benevolent, why do innocent people suffer? God must be able to be aware that this is happening, and being all-powerful, he must be able to prevent it. Being benevolent, he must want to prevent it. Why, then, does such suffering exist?[3]

One of the West's big ideas has been the idea of human freedom.

According to this idea, God does not prevent suffering because to do so would limit human freedom. Lev Shestov read this argument as a limitation on God, and his passionate cry that for God anything is possible was the cry of one who will continue to challenge God. Like Job, he defined his integrity in terms of empathy and justice, and he refused to accept that God is incapable of, or refuses, a similar integrity.

A key text for Shestov and other existentialists is Dostoevsky's *The Brothers Karamazov*. The story Shestov refers to repeatedly is the parable "The Grand Inquisitor"; told by Ivan, it addresses human capacity for evil, the suffering of innocents, and the absence of God. Ivan, it will be recalled, expresses the voice of European Enlightenment. He takes the position of the detached observer who attempts to ground his moral ideals in reason rather than faith. He speaks from a desire for perfection and from a stance that is both detached from, and rests on, a sense of moral superiority.

In arguing his case, Ivan tells numerous stories of the everyday torture of children. One such story concerns a powerful aristocratic general who had on his property thousands of serfs. He also had kennels full of dogs and a hundred dog boys to take care of them. One day a serf boy injures a dog, and the general has the boy taken from his mother and locked up overnight. In the morning, the general comes out in full retinue—horses, hounds, dog boys, huntsmen, all ready for the chase. The child is stripped naked and forced to run, and the general sets the hounds on him. As the boy runs the hounds catch him and tear him to pieces before his mother's eyes.[4]

Ivan is arguing with the monk Alyosha, and he says, "With my pitiful, earthly, Euclidian understanding, all I know is that there is suffering and that there are none guilty; that effect follows cause, simply and directly; that everything flows and finds its level. . . . I must have justice, or I will destroy myself."[5] Ivan is addressing the perennial Western question of suffering, and his analysis leads him to nihilism. He outlines several possibilities: if suffering exists because the sins of the fathers are visited on the children, then God is unjust. If God is beyond comprehension, then torture may sometimes be good. If the afterlife is meant to make up for suffering, "then it would appear that divine justice holds that it is all right to torture children provided you give them some candy afterwards."[6] Ivan ends up devising a complete double bind: if God exists and permits such suffering, then God is cruel and there is no justice in the universe. If God does not exist, the mechanistic view of the universe must be true, and "the universe consists of nothing but meaningless material objects in causal interaction. . . . People are determined to do what they do, no one is guilty of anything, and so there are no such things as right or wrong." Understandably, he finds both accounts of the cosmos equally intolerable. For Ivan, there is no reason to go on living.[7]

Shestov reads the Enlightenment position as saying that man's freedom to choose between good and evil takes precedence over God's capacity to prevent suffering and to save the innocent; the philosopher cries out in anguish at what he sees as a debasement of man and God, compassion and justice. Like Job, he refuses to reconcile himself to horrors, and like Job, he continues to hold out the possibility of dialogue.[8]

Job, too, was asking these questions, and he, too, refused to submit to the idea that suffering could be justified by reference to a higher good. What Job wanted was for God to come out from hiding. When God did speak to Job he offered nothing that could be thought to explain his actions in allowing Job to suffer. Shestov was writing before the Holocaust, and while he was in no doubt about man's capacity to inflict suffering, he did not have to face the Holocaust and ask where God had been. In contrast, Elie Wiesel, a Holocaust survivor, speaks quite differently about Job, reading the story through the experience of the death world in his essay "Job: Our Contemporary." Wiesel admires Job's rebellion, his insistence that God speak with him, and his refusal to justify suffering on the grounds that it must be deserved. He considers the curious ending of the Job story—the ending in which everything is restored to Job, and he lives happily ever after: "I prefer to think that the Book's true ending was lost. That Job died without having repented, without having humiliated himself; that he succumbed to his grief an uncompromising and whole man." Wiesel understands Job precisely as a contemporary. "I was preoccupied with Job, especially in the early years after the war," Wiesel writes. "In those days he could be seen on every road of Europe. Wounded, robbed, mutilated. Certainly not happy. Nor resigned."[9]

Wiesel concludes his passionate meditative essay by speaking the questions he wanted Job to have asked: "He should have said to God: Very well, I forgive You, I forgive You to the extent of my sorrow, my anguish. But what about my dead children, do they forgive You? What right have I to speak on their behalf? . . . By accepting Your inequities, do I not become your accomplice? Now it is my turn to choose between You and my children, and I refuse to repudiate them. I demand that justice be done to them, if not to me, and that the trial continue."[10] Wiesel distrusts Job's abdication to God's view, and he concludes: "Job personified man's eternal quest for justice and truth. . . . [T]hanks to him, we know that it is given to man to transform divine injustice into human justice and compassion."[11]

Making a Death World

In September 1980, I was just beginning my research at Yarralin. On the twelfth of that month, a light fixed-wing aircraft flew low over the community and dropped dingo bait. It was the poison 1080, and as people there knew, it is regarded as extremely dangerous because there is no known antidote. The method in broadacre baiting is that chunks of dried meat are laced with 1080 and dropped at regular intervals by plane. The poison is toxic to many animals in high doses, and species other than canines are at risk. Furthermore, any animal that eats the remains of an animal that has been poisoned is at risk—this includes eagles, hawks, and crows, as well as other dingoes. The poison remains in animal bones for up to two years, so the threat to other animals lingers long after the original poisoning event.[12]

The Aboriginal people in Yarralin were outraged that dingo bait had been dropped on their country. Their concerns covered a range of issues: protection of dingoes and camp dogs, protection of other animals, protection of children, and control over their own land. The land issue was aggravated by the fact that the land area that was theirs under Anglo-Australian law was much smaller than the total land that was theirs under their own system. Almost all of the traditional homelands are now under pastoral tenure. Regardless of Anglo-Australian tenure, people were acutely aware that dingo bait had been dropped all over their traditional country, and in their community as well. For clarity it needs to be added that as far as is known, the dingo bait was being dropped by the adjacent pastoralist.

Old Tim Yilngayarri, the oldest of the Dingo lawmen, asked me to write a letter: "Tell the white man, 'don't touch any Aboriginal land. . . . Aboriginal people got to stay on their own land, and keep their own law.'" Somewhat more ominously, he told me a little story: "There was a man who shot dogs, and he's dead now." For clarity it needs to be stated that the man who shot dogs was reported to have killed eighty or more dogs in what was clearly a dog shooting of the kind described in chapter 2. Old Tim's story—that the man is now dead—sounded like a threat, but as it turned out in the exploration of the story, it was actually a kind of promise, or statement of causality: if *A* then *B*. You kill dogs, you die. That's how it is.

As discussed in chapter 6, the pastoralists' position is that dingo control is essential for protecting calves. Scientific evidence indicates that the pastoralists' view is misguided, but this is new knowledge, not readily available in 1980. But whether right or wrong in relation to protecting calves, aerial dingo baiting is premised on imagining a country without dingoes and setting out to accomplish it. It carries the further implication that all the "collateral damage"—the deaths of many other animals—is morally irrelevant.

Yarralin people protested. Within their own traditional law, people have autonomous responsibility over their own country. Dingo baiting violated that law, but the wrong goes deeper, pressing violently against the foundational moral principle that a country and its living beings take care of their own (see chapter 2). To be in connection is to take care and to be cared for. Country is not just the homeland for humans, but the homeland for all the living things that are there, and care is circulated through country in cross-species relationships of responsibility and accountability. The care of each part of a given country contributes to other parts and thus to sustaining connectivities. Using ecological terms, we would say that country is a self-organizing system within which living beings truly stand or fall together. To live powerfully in the world requires people to act responsibly within the relationships in which their own lives are enmeshed. Care of one's country, one's people, one's Dreaming sites, and one's nonhuman kin are some of the actions through which people sustain, and are themselves sustained by, relationships of mutual interdependence.

Life and death in country are always in connection; and so we are invited to consider what it means to be in connection, to have one's interests entangled in the interests of others. To think within a paradigm of connectivity is to imagine that living beings are always enmeshed in a shared moral domain that is dedicated to life's becoming. The dingo-baiting episode violated connectivity along numerous parameters. In this area, 1080 is used specifically to kill dingoes, so from the perspective of Dingo people, the attack on dingoes was an attack on them as well as on their dingo relations. Perhaps even more devastatingly, not only life but also death was under attack. Dingo baiting spread death around the place so that living things who came for sustenance might actually be harmed or killed. To the extent that food was disguised as poison, mutual care was perverted. This violent work disguised death as life; it wrenched the process of life away from flourishing mutuality and toward indiscriminate death. And death itself was perverted, since an animal that had been poisoned would become food for other animals and would poison them as well. 1080 instigates waves of death. No longer is life making and unmaking itself in country. The unmaking is taking over. Rather than death being turned back toward life, it is amplifying.

Death Narratives

Recent philosophical literature is marked by a growing interest in death, and increasingly there is an interest in the community qualities of death. James Hatley is a key figure here. He works with the death narrative concept in his insightful analysis of man-made mass death. In human terms, the death narrative situates death and the dead within a historical community. Hatley explains that the death narrative is set within time, and involves the transmission of wisdom, memory, and traditions that are passed from generation to generation (see chapter 2). A given group "can be seen as a wave of memory, insight, and expectation coursing through time, a wave

that lifts up and sustains the individuals of each succeeding generation, even as those individuals make their own particular contribu-
tions to or modifications of that wave."[13] He writes: "Situated in the
difference between death and birth, one is addressed by the lives one
inherits. These lives inspire one, literally, breathe into one one's own
possibility of existence. Yet the existence one receives in this inspiration does not belong to one's forebears, precisely because the very
terms of its inspiration is a transitive crossing-over that generates a
new existence characterized in terms of a new responsibility."[14]

The catastrophic will-to-destruction that finds fulfillment in the
death world violently attacks the community within which death offers inspiration. A death world is a place of cascading destruction
involving both time and life. Hatley's death-narrative concept clari-
fies the catastrophic quality of this death work.[15] On the scale of generations, wisdom, memory, and traditions are passed along waves of
successive life; and so mass-death seeks to eradicate these gifts and
these responsibilities. Death work is a will toward totality: it refuses
the call of others. Death work "acts as if it were its own creator, as if
it might never die, as if the other's suffering meant nothing at all to
it, as if everything were possible."[16] This may be an attempt to turn
history into a narcissistic mirror, Hatley contends: "One writes the
past and future as a mode of colonisation. All the other times are
resources for one's own."[17] And this colonizing endeavor is part of
an utterly delusional as if: as if others don't matter, as if there are no
limits. Death work thus attacks time and the generative quality of
death. Killers use death in their search to collapse all time and all life
into their own totalizing domain.

Hatley suggests an ecological dimension to the death narrative
concept, but he does not develop it because his focus is on the human dimension.[18] I expand ecological perspectives in two directions—first into conversation with Western science and then into
conversation with an Indigenous ontology of connectivity. Where
Western science seeks to universalize, Aboriginal philosophy situates life, death, gift, and responsibility in country. Both perspectives
matter.

We have seen that Hatley speaks of groups or species as waves
coursing through time. Similarly, Margulis and Sagan speak of life
as "a material process shifting and surfing over matter like a strange

slow wave."[19] According to Margulis and Sagan, life is a becoming, a process set in time. Life expands complexity through time in the context of a universal kinship, such that all living beings are ultimately related to each other through their shared substance, their conjoined histories, and their embeddedness in the eons of life's time on Earth.[20] Thus "life's body is a veneer of growing and self-interacting matter encasing Earth."[21]

Margulis and Sagan draw out two lessons here: The first is that "our destiny is joined to that of other species."[22] The second is that life on Earth is not ours to reject or destroy.[23] Implicit in this analysis is the claim that the delusional *as if* is a fundamental error. The error involves unmaking the world of life, *as if* there were no limits, *as if* there were some other world to be gained. They go on to say that all life has two lives—the one we are given and the one we make.[24] In light of Hatley's work, we need to add a third. The third life is the one we bequeath to others. Structurally, the bequeathed life is simply the given for a new generation, but because life is set within irreversible time, we gain a better understanding both of ourselves and of life processes when we consider our participation in all three lives: that which is given, that which is lived, and that which will be bequeathed. Life desires that each living being (perhaps excepting some bacteria) live all three. This means that life desires that individual lives become gifts to others.

The wreckage of catastrophe, the death work designed to produce emptiness, cuts across life's desire, working against the grain of life's flourishing diversity, plowing ever more furrows of death. The genius of Benjamin's ninth thesis, itself a poetic distillation of generations of thinking about history, is to show with sudden and vivid imagery the wreckage that results from the justification of suffering in the name of progress. Catastrophe and wreckage are not byproducts or collateral damage; the better world toward which ideas of progress direct themselves is nowhere to be seen; the work of the moment is disaster piled upon disaster: the "pile of debris" that is still growing skyward.[25]

Nothing better communicates the massive power that sustains the delusion of progress, that myopic *as if* that says that everything is fine, than the visible and immediate catastrophes it generates. Long, slow, and relatively invisible catastrophes are now the homeland of our lives, but often we are not aware of that. The visible catastrophes are accessible to us, and they demonstrate that disaster falls on all of us, humans and the others. The Australian poet Stephen Edgar writes of this zone of multiple disasters in his poem on Chernobyl.

2 The Dogs

At first confused, distressed,
They scrabbled to get aboard the departing buses,
Then followed the exhaust,
Back windows where they saw the children's faces

And frantic fading hands.
Abandoned to the zone of their contagion,
A town emptied of sounds
And lights and human acts, a haunted region

Through which in trails of scent
The ghosts of their lost owners went parading
Their presence like a taunt,
They grew afraid, suspicious, wild, marauding

In a demented pack,
Eating the cats (also of course forsaken),
Attacking any stock
Still left at large, or tethered, terror-stricken,

Till finally reduced
To scavenge—in a sort of savage justice—
Rubbish and household waste,
The last they would inherit from their masters.

And then gun-bearing men
Came, cloaked like apparitions in strange clothing,
To hunt and shoot them down
And keep close watch until they stopped their writhing.

But after they had gone
Some of the dogs—according to the rumour—
Escaped from the dead zone,
Spreading, like spring into the coming summer,

To the otherworld of dream,
Where children reach out to assuage their hungers—
Some to be savaged, some
To feel a tongue against their outstretched fingers.[26]

Disasters make and define multispecies communities of fate, both in faith and in dishonor. This is to say that an important way to define communities is not by national or "natural" (species) boundaries, but by shared vulnerability and shared suffering.[27] The consolation of poetry, for Edgar, is to propose interspecies relationships of continuity and affection, like those we have encountered with Bobby, Youngfella, and Blackie. Some Chernobyl dogs, astoundingly enough, may still want to offer affection. In chapter 11, I return to discussions of love. Here the point to be developed is that of shared vulnerability.

Country

Science tells a story that is grounded in the particular, often the micro- or macroscopic, and at the same time is generalized beyond specific contexts. In contrast, Indigenous ecologies are embedded and embodied in country. As we have seen, country is the matrix of all the living beings and all the life-systems that interactively share that time and place. At best, country is a zone of connectivities organizing itself toward mutually flourishing interdependencies. My Aboriginal teachers would insist that country participates in death narratives, that they do not emerge solely or primarily from interhuman engagements. In the context of country, the flourishing of life is the narrative of the preceding generations. Flourishing country exists because of all the living things that contributed to the life of the country. The ecological narrative of country embeds death in processes through which it is turned back toward life.

From the perspective of country, the death narrative concept encompasses the idea that death binds living beings into an ecological community; this is not just a historical community as in a strictly human context, but rather is a larger living and localized community. It follows that in areas of mass environmental destruction the future of one's death collapses as the future of flourishing ecosystems collapses. Where death was meant to turn back toward life, as life itself collapses there is less and less toward which death can be turned.[28] We have seen the parallel in the story of Job: amplification of death initiated a process of ruination of people's deaths along with their lives. Ecological catastrophe accomplishes the same cascading ruination of both past and future life and death. We see here an amplification such that the balance between life and death is overturned, and death starts piling up corpses in the land of the living. The delusional *as if* is turning living countries into death worlds—places where entire generations of living things and connectivities are being destroyed.

Such are the recursive and amplifying effects of the will-to-destruction. Remember that ominous story: "There was a man who shot dogs, and he's dead now." The story starts to resonate as the fate and destiny of those who indiscriminately spread death. What becomes of humans when the partners to our humanity are gone? What becomes of us when the webs that sustain us and others are subjected to expanding death work?

Trophies

Traveling the outback, one often sees dead dingoes. Some are run down by vehicles; some are dead from unknown but not unknowable causes. Many, perhaps most, have been the victim of the poison 1080 and have suffered terribly before dying.[29] I was traveling across a cattle station in the Northern Territory once to visit a few sacred sites. We had stopped to look at trees that were the transformations of Dreaming creators, and we had talked about how the trees and the people keep going together through generations. Perhaps it was the smell of death that first alerted us to another presence. We found it soon enough—a dingo that had been killed and hung over the fence. It looked at first as if the dingo might have been trying to jump the fence to get away; this was clearly an odd notion, but one struggles to make sense of events such as this. On closer examination, we realized that the dead body had been casually but carefully draped across the fence. Was it a message, and if so, to whom was it addressed?

I asked a friend who knows pastoralists better than I do what she thought the person might have been saying in putting the body on display, and she said, "He does it because he can." It seems as good an explanation as one is likely to get. He may do it because he hates dingoes, he may do it because he thinks it is some kind of message to other dingoes, or perhaps to other humans, to Aboriginal people, perhaps, who call dingoes Mother and Father. But in the end, what is on display is that he can do this.

In this vile perversion, the dingo's death is offered as part of the killer's history and community. In life, these creatures were despised by the pastoralist, and now the death is displayed in a narrative of total power. The pastoralist wants to destroy the animals, and he wants to display his dominance. This dingo, this outlaw, can be defiled with relative impunity. Social power as well as interspecies power is on display here.

This exhibit offers up trophies in the war against the wild and living world. I want to know: What power do we think we gain when we steal the future of other living things, perverting their future and their history toward what might be taken to be human purposes?

"His face is turned toward the past. . . . The pile of debris grows skyward." Near Kidman Springs Research Station, Northern Territory, 2006. (AUTHOR'S PHOTO)

And is it not evident that such totalizing delusions are tipping the balance between making and unmaking in favor of runaway systems of disconnection and disorder?

These questions bring me back to the Angel of History. I am imagining her as a wild dog. I hear her howling with all the complex vocabulary of her kind. She is calling out to try to find her companions, not only dingoes but humans as well.

The quality of this cry is complex. We have heard other cries, human cries, more and more of them all the time, and perhaps we wonder if we owe the same moral response to animals. The Canadian philosopher Ian Hacking discusses this question in an insightful review essay on Coetzee's *The Lives of Animals* and *Disgrace*. Hacking gives particular attention to *The Lives of Animals,* discussing the comparison Elizabeth Costello draws between animal slaughter and the slaughter of human beings (specifically Jewish human beings under the Nazi regime). He observes, as do characters in the book, that this view causes extreme discomfort. The character Abraham Stern contests this view most vigorously. Hacking writes, "Of course I agree with Abraham Stern: 'If Jews were treated like cattle, it does not follow that cattle are treated like Jews. The inversion insults the memory of the dead.'" Having said he agrees with this position, Hacking continues, "Yet I cannot formulate, to my own satisfaction, what is wrong with [the] rhetoric. Coetzee is not being cheap."[30]

The wild dog Angel can offer insight. The problem may not hinge precisely or solely on the specific cruelty of the deaths, or on the species being subjected to the death work, so much as it may hinge on the complexities of death work. I would not deny that cruelty is immensely important, but such an emphasis may be too narrowly focused on physical suffering.[31] Catastrophe inheres in the destructive unmaking of the world of life that has been making itself so beautifully for so long. The world that is bequeathed to us is, in our hands and in our time, being unmade. And there is more: in unmaking this gifted world, death work unmakes time, and totalizes its annihilating grasp on life's future and diversity. And more: the future complex richness of life—our potential gift to the future—is being eradicated.

If the Angel of History were a dog, she would be in the world, in relationship, in communication, and she would be calling out. Let us say that this is so; let us continue with the idea that the world is real and that others communicate, and that we too are called into connection. This Angel is howling now because her fellow human creatures have lost themselves in the labyrinths of their own death world and seem not to know how to find their way out. She is howling with grief over the deaths and the torture, and the relentlessness of it all, and she is calling out in search, trying to pull us and others back into connectivity. "Come back," she calls, "come back to the world of the living."

In the midst of this death world we are called to embrace the forces of life that bring us into being and nurture us. To respond to this call would be to make the turn toward the lives of others, a turn that would put limits on our own delusional *as if* actions. The dramas of recognition and encounter engendered in response to such calls bring us face-to-face with the death narratives whose breath has given us life. These are narratives that honor both life and death, honor the balance, and honor life's deep desire for connectivities. Our situatedness in time and place suggests that the *future,* too, may call out to us, seeking the inspiriting force that only we can breathe into it.

Near Kosciusko National Park, New South Wales, 2006. (AUTHOR'S PHOTO)

9. Ruined Faces

After Jessica told me about the dingo tree I went to see it, and after I had seen it I started writing about it. As I presented my writings in various places, people became aware of my interest and shared more information with me. One evening a friend of a friend brought some photos around to the house. The more I looked at them, the more I was struck by a peculiarity that took some time to decipher. There is the overwhelming response that dogs should not be hung in trees, so the photo is necessarily difficult. But in these photos there was more, and perhaps I just couldn't believe what I was seeing: these dogs had been skinned. They were all meat and bones, teeth and skull, but no skins. No skins at all, except for their little socks which the killer had left intact.

I want to stand with these unbearably defenseless bodies, and with the memory that they had been living creatures. Suffering matters; everyone who has suffered knows that it does. As I gaze at these distressed bodies I think: even if this was all done after death, even if there was no suffering, I know myself to be encountering violent unmaking. How shall we come face-to-face with these, our fellow creatures? Even to ask this question is to be reminded that once having encountered a place of unmaking, there is no going back. One is already and forever implicated.

The Unmaking

Doggers are said to display dead dogs in order to show that they are doing their work well. They display the bodies, and presumably they also skin them. I am looking at these naked bodies, and now I remember that the torture and killing of predators is a hideously familiar story in the Western world, and elsewhere as well, as Barry Lopez discusses so insightfully.[1] The bodies are trophies, and thus are mirrors: they give us ourselves. They give us ourselves as we are when we go out to torture and kill, and are proud of our work.

In the context of human torture and genocide, Elaine Scarry, James Hatley, and others write of doubled suffering: first the victim is harmed, and then the victim is deprived of the capacity to assert that this harm matters.[2] Elie Wiesel, who himself experienced the interior of the death world, writes, "It must be emphasized that the victims suffered more, and more profoundly, from the indifference of on-lookers than from the brutality of the executioner."[3] Indifference may seem passive, but in the context of suffering it is best understood as the refusal of relationship, the refusal of an ethical call. As we have seen with Job, one form of refusal is justification: it is the assertion that the suffering is deserved; it seeks to bring suffering back into the realm of rationality or conventional theodicy. It is an active reinscription of a boundary of exclusion.

Dingo trees amplify suffering further. The trophy display seems to require the victims to state that the harm has been a positive good in the world, that somehow their suffering and death are something for the killers to have been proud of. Such displays remind us that our history is replete with these displays of power. Crucifixion is perhaps the most widely known, and in its complexity is something of a template for varied imaginings of relationships between death and power. Power in this context is claimed for the greater good. The dingo tree puts Hegel's slaughterhouse of history on display beside the road, offering a tally of winners and losers. Trophies form a "narcissistic mirror"[4] in which the killers can read their own moral superiority, for it is they who have made the world a better place.

As I work back and forth between the philosophy of Old Tim Yilngayarri and that of Emmanuel Levinas, I am focusing on the face-to-face encounter with dead bodies, and with the cry of alarm that asks where God is in all of this. I heard this call in my own voice; it was mine. And yet it goes way outside the self to become a call for connection arising out of the loss of *both* other and self that one experiences in an encounter with irreparable harm.

The Kinship

In Aboriginal creation stories, the life of Earth is always coming forth, and always on the move. Creation is the work of the Dreaming beings who emerged from the ground and who walked and shaped the Earth (see chapter 2). They walked, they created, and they returned into the ground, and so the ground we now walk upon is the source of life. As well, it is the recipient of death, and it is Earth itself that holds and nurtures the movement between death and life.

Cross-species kin groups are founded in flesh and blood, and what happens to any member of the group impacts other members of the group. There is vulnerability in these relationships because of the connectivities, and at the same time there is strength. No one (human or nonhuman) stands or falls alone, and at the same time no one is exempt from the suffering of others. Dingoes are part of the Dreaming or totemic way of life-in-country, and so they are part of the sacred geography. There are tracks and sites, stories, songs, designs, and ceremonies. Where Dreaming Dingoes traveled, those tracks and sites are in the country of particular people; these people are the Lawmen and Lawwomen. They uphold Dingo life and law. Dingo people's first responsibility is to their dingo kin and to the sites, songs, and ceremonies. Dingo ancestors are not undifferentiated, and neither are the people. The late Anzac and Hector were brothers and senior members of one of the Dingo kin groups I lived with. They described their ancestors as two Dingoes, each with his own personal name. These Dingoes' markings include a "white face, white collar, and four white stockings."[5]

Standing before the death tree, I can't help but think of Anzac and Hector. I look at the ground, at the twisted remains of leg bones and vertebrae, and I imagine the blood soaking deeper and deeper, congealing perhaps into an anguished cry to which Old Tim, Anzac, and Hector would always be responsive. They are their brothers' keepers.

Birth of the Human

Old Tim had lived through events I can barely imagine; massacres, extinctions, working conditions that were close to slavery, nearly complete abrogation of his human rights, and under the control of people who did not include the nonhuman world in its system of ethics. During all the long decades from about 1905 to 1970, he kept faith with his own law and his own way of participatory life-in-country.

In our region, he was notorious for his jillions of dogs. They were camp dogs, nothing special in any way, shape, or form, but they and Old Tim were devoted to each other. One of his favorite stories was about the time that he and his wife, Mary Rutungali, got stranded in the bush. They had been in the neighboring community of Daguragu, about 60 miles (100 kilometers) from Yarralin, and nobody would give them a ride home (perhaps because of the dogs) so they set out cross-country, on foot with dogs. This would have been about 1977, when they were both in their seventies. At some point, Tim's legs gave out, and they had to make camp at a water bore and wait out the wet season. They were able to survive because their dogs hunted and brought them food. Eventually some Whitefellas found them and wanted to know who they were. Characteristically, Tim wouldn't give them a straight answer. He laughed with a crazy joy as he related a conversation between himself and a bore mechanic in which he cagily refused to tell the man what had happened. "Where you come from?" the White man asked. "Aaah, well, I come from desert country, from valley country, from the long grass! What about you?" Old Tim replied, with more than a hint of postcolonial critique. After more conversation of this kind, the White man concluded, "I think you're crazy." Old Tim finished the story by saying, "Aaah, we made him laugh, that Whitefella."

When Old Tim told creation stories, he told them with humor and with the authority of place-based knowledge (hinted at obliquely in his reply to the bore mechanic). He spoke with vivid attention to detail and with the passion of knowing and telling a story that takes us to the heart of the meaning of our lives. If philosophy is the search for "what matters most," Old Tim's stories went straight into it.[6] Originally, Old Tim said, people and dogs were all one creature:

> In the beginning, when we came out of the ground, we had a long nose like a dog. Dreaming dog came around and looked, and reckoned, "Hey, you've done it wrong!" Long nose, big mouth, Dreaming was doing it wrong. Beginning Dreaming was working then. He didn't like his head like a dog. He wanted it to be round. He made a round one out of honeybee wax. And he called the little bat, that's the doctor, the little bat, and the bat said, "You come to me." He fixed their genitals up then—girls got a vulva, and boys got things

rearranged. That's the beginning Dreaming that did all this. Same
for women, same for boys. Now everything was good.

His story about the creation of humans in their human shape reso-
nates with other Dreaming stories and yet also differs from them.
Old Tim told it as a universal history of humanity (see chapter 1).
Dogs are ancestors and kin of everyone: Mother and Father Dingo
for Aboriginal people, and white dogs as the Mother and Father of
white people.

The Shadow of Death

The God who delivered Israel out of Egypt did not come to
Auschwitz. The question, "Where is God?" haunts the Western
world and has had a profound effect on the West's scholarship.[7]
God's absence in the face of inconceivably terrible man-made mass
death poses problems for both God and humanity. Like Old Tim,
Emmanuel Levinas lived through events that I can barely imagine:
World War II, incarceration in a Nazi "camp," loss of family, and
later achievement of prestige as a French intellectual. Compared to
the great post-Holocaust theologians such as Emil Fackenheim and
Richard Rubenstein, Levinas does not explicitly center his work on
the Holocaust. His words echo Dostoevsky's Ivan when he writes,
"If there is an explicitly Jewish moment in my thought, it is the reference to Auschwitz, where God let the Nazis do what they wanted.
Consequently, what remains? Either this means that there is no reason for morality and hence it can be concluded that everyone should
act like the Nazis, or the moral law maintains its authority. . . . Can
we speak of morality after the failure of morality?"[8]

Before turning toward the question of what authority might
remain, I want to sojourn briefly again with the Bobby essay. My
thoughts are speculative, but they haunt me: I cannot reconcile myself with Levinas's own silence. God's silencing of the dogs on the
night of the Exodus meant that on God's night of terror the dogs
were witness to the death work; they were hidden, perhaps, in darkness, and they communicated through silence rather than through
voice. The witness who is silent and hidden is a powerful figure for
imagining the intent of Levinas's comments on the apparent collu-

sion between God and the Nazis. Recall that Bobby didn't do Nazi work, either as a brutal guard or as an indifferent bystander; the collaboration, as Levinas hints at it, was between God and the Nazis on one side, and prisoners and Bobby on the other side. And yet, Levinas rejected Bobby because he didn't have the brain to universalize his maxims. I wonder, at times, if Levinas found that he himself didn't have it in him to universalize his maxims. What universality could possibly hold sway from within the "nowhere" place[9] where "God let the Nazis do what they wanted"? What maxims, arising out of the experience of somewhere that is "nowhere," can logos exercise its brain with? Bobby's long shadow offers not authority but protection. In that shadow of security there is an astonishingly complex and elusive space of witness. The good dog with the long, dark shadow gives shelter: to each and every witness dog, silent in the night, Levinas included.

Returning to a more text-based approach to these questions, the Australian philosopher Michael Fagenblat writes that Levinas's ethics carries "an almost secret reference to the real authority behind the face, be it God or the impersonal 'third.'"[10] Levinas approaches this problem through relationship. "Self is not substance but relation," he writes in his discussion of Martin Buber.[11] The particular formula—substance versus relationship—is, in Levinas's view, shared by numerous thinkers, and he himself appears to agree. Immediately we see that in promoting relationship he is rejecting Western atomistic thought. There is no singular self, but only self-and-other. The emphasis on relationship over substance can be understood as a move away from the view of an inward-focused essential self, and toward an open, permeable, relational self. As we have seen in chapter 3, however, the very abstractness and arbitrariness of Levinas's views of the other call forth the question of any self's corporeal, vulnerable existence.

We may now pause to consider some of the implications of the idea that self is not substance. In the aftermath of the Holocaust, people had good reason to be wary of categories based on biogenetic substance. Levinas explicitly rejects the idea that racism is a "biological concept."[12] This is no doubt true, but it is also true that concepts of biogenetic substance have been mobilized to sustain the boundary on one side of which are humans deemed to be life-worthy and on the other side of which are those deemed not to be life-worthy. European culture has for millennia projected issues of life and death onto the body, and defined life-worthiness in terms of categories that we label "race."[13] Clearly, the self defined by substance is in terrible peril in a world where substance is the criterion by which decisions about life-worthiness are made. A turn away from substance and toward relationship is entirely understandable. And yet, the process of abstracting relation from substance can also be understood as another form of violence, as Irigaray has shown. Through abstractions the *other*—the source of the call that brings us into our own selfhood—becomes itself an abstract category, a nearly empty space. Similarly, Fagenblat identifies this emptiness as the great peril of Levinas's ethics: he "ends up with an ethics that is so impassive, indeed formal, that it risks itself becoming pure theory."[14]

Levinas's response to the question "Where is God?" is that God may be encountered in relationship, yes, but we encounter only the trace. God himself, herself, itself, has receded to a plane of transcendence that is beyond us. Levinas gives us a God so abstract as to be effectively absent, and calls us to be responsive to a face that is equally abstract, disconnected from any living body. Let us imagine that the face is so abstract because it is a mask. And let us imagine that behind the mask are the hidden others of Levinas's life-work: the 6 million dead. Think of his work as survivor writing, as a body of philosophical and theological thought that forms a drawn-out Kaddish for the people who died and for the God who let it happen. "Self is not substance but relation": if we imagine that in his life-world the other who calls self into being is a ghost, then we can understand that perhaps there is no substance with which to connect. And if we imagine that people glimpse a flicker of God in relationships, it is the God that is rapidly departing, perhaps leaving this world for good, perhaps accompanying the dead, perhaps already a ghost himself.

The first commandment for Levinas is "Thou Shalt Not Kill."[15] He speaks into the Holocaust Death World, where even the dead bodies were eradicated, and he speaks in response to a call that arises from the Earth itself, like the blood of Abel. Levinas refuses to be Cain, and so he must always be responsive to his brother, even in death. And these are the dead who were killed precisely so that their people should have no future, so that their deaths as well as their lives should be obliterated.[16]

The self who hears their call is brought into relationship already having survived, already hearing a call that is losing substance, that is slipping into emptiness. The living want to call out to them, begging them to come back, and wanting to remember them forever. In this survivor's world, we are always doubly in debt because they are the doubly dead. And so all those beautiful tropes are ghostly and insubstantial, full of love, and drenched in hidden grief. In this reading, Levinas testifies to the unimaginable: to lost bodies, lost lives, lost dead, lost humanity, and the lost God.

Wild Dogs

Recall that Old Tim spoke of how Dingoes made humans, universalizing the story by saying that Aboriginal people come out of dingoes, and White people come out of white dogs. He spoke about how dogs are bewildered by the lack of reciprocity between humans and dogs and distressed at their mistreatment: "I made them man and woman. Now you've dropped me, put me in the rubbish dump" (see chapter 6). As if to drive home the significance of reciprocity, Old Tim offered a statement that for me is one of his greatest challenges: "True God! God's a man: Lord Jesus!"

With this statement, Old Tim tells us that God is here on Earth. God is human, and humans are descended from Dingoes, therefore God too is descended from a dog. I do not know all that Tim may have meant with the term "God," but in saying that God's a man he brought Christianity to Earth and situated God among us not as a being arrived from elsewhere but as a being born of this Earth. He is another wild-dog human, yet another son of a "b" who shares in the Earthly life we live so exuberantly.

Old Tim was not enmeshed in visions of a supreme, monotheistic transcendent God. I suspect that he had no idea how theologically difficult his words would be. I am not actually suggesting that he was offering a theology, but whatever it was that he offered, he delighted in it. In the spirit of delight, I want to "tell on and on," giving his words a slow and recursive reading, and continuing the delight by referring to his pronouncement as a dogsology.

God the man lives and dies as a human, and thus he returns according to the Dingo law. That law cycles people through other animals. There is no way to return to the human world without first experiencing life as another kind of animal. And so we are challenged to open our minds to god the wild dog, the kangaroo, goanna, bird, crocodile (see chapter 7). In doing so, we move toward a path that takes us away from a theological dilemma that has been outlined succinctly, albeit with the subtlety of a sledgehammer, by Emil Fackenheim. He argues that a transcendent God is irrelevant because it is indiscriminately inaccessible, but equally, an immanent God is irrelevant because it is indiscriminately accessible.[17] Both visions rest on an underlying unity—either God is wholly other, or God is wholly everything. Panentheism, the view that God is both immanent and transcendent, appears to bridge these oppositions; Rigby's elegant analysis of panentheism and its place in the context of the European Romantic imagination is suggestive of points of convergence,[18] and yet I remain cautious about slipping into any concepts of unity. Old Tim's dogsology fractures both unities. To say that God's a man is to say that God participates in the human condition. Sometimes he is human, sometimes not, sometimes clever, sometimes not. There is always an element of uncertainty; we can't know for sure which person or animal is god at any moment. This metamorphic god, neither wholly nor always any given thing, calls for a theological precautionary principle. In the absence of knowing exactly who or what god is at any given moment, wisdom would be found in considering that he could be anything.

A slow reading of Old Tim's dogsology gives us mystery. He was not saying that god is all men, or all life. At any moment, the question of who or where god is will of necessity be unanswerable. Indeed, as long as god may be another, god may also be us. Perhaps Old Tim was god. All we know is that god is somewhere here in this living system. This is a quantum god: attempts to pinpoint god once and for all within the system will forever elude us. Here, in this slow reading of the very short story "God's a man," we find not the trace of a departing god but the always possibility of god coming forth. That cry of alarm, *Where are you?* might emerge differently from within Old Tim's dogsology. Face-to-face with the death tree, one might cry: *Dear God, was this you?* And even as the question developed, one would know that it was too late. It is true that one sees in the dingo tree the possibility of god's cruel death. Equally, one sees processes of extermination and extinction. In these processes, the possibilities for god, as for all of us, become fewer because life is being deprived of future generations.[19] Thus while the possibility of killing god seems terrible, Old Tim's dogsology acknowledges that god dies and comes back, dies and comes back. In a world in which life depends on death, god too has to die. Death is not god's enemy. But in the current cascade of extinctions that has become the sixth great extinction event on Earth, god's future is being killed. Today the question is not "Was this you?" but the even more unbearable question: "Will you be able to keep coming forth?"

Ruination

"Ruins do not lie," the brilliant scholar of trauma Maria Tumarkin tells us. She quotes the Sarajevan writer Semezdin Mehmedinoviæ: "The shells that come down on the National Bank have created a distinct stone relief on its façade: reality is recognised in its wholeness only as it shatters to bits."[20] The dingo death tree is a site of ruination, a chip off the wider disaster of anthropogenic extinctions. One of the realities it reveals through the shattered bodies is that the animals are required to testify to the killers' pride in death work.

I wanted to know what had happened to the skins of this "strange fruit," and here again, Jessica was my guide. She and her family go fishing in this area, and she suggested that I visit the general store in a small town called Wee Jasper. There on the wall were dingo skins, fox skins, and the skins of dogs. Dingoes and dogs were classed together and sold for one hundred dollars each, fox skins for forty dollars. They were displayed in the store along with the cold drinks, ice creams, and groceries. I asked the young lady behind the counter if they sold many, and she said yes. I asked if she knew what people wanted them for, and she shuddered and said she supposed they wanted to hang them on their walls at home.

As the dogs are dismembered, the ruin is spread out beyond the tree. Every time we encounter pieces we come face-to-face with shattered selves, shattered relationships, and the possibility, again and again, of shattered God. We see the ongoing shame: that violence between humans and other animals is so terribly one-sided. We see that we are called to witness and to act, and we cannot help but recall that dingoes are endangered animals, and that we are in the midst of so many extinctions.

The ruined bodies of dead dingoes confront us with terrible truths. The Australian poet Peter Boyle writes that dogs can be seen to be:

> reaching out beyond where we can reach. The pitch of their howling addresses the stars. In this they move beyond us.
> Equally the wordlessness of what they say as they howl may give their lamentation an authenticity our own clumsy grappling with speech blocks from us.
> Those species of dog especially who must grapple with the threat of extinction might be seen as simply going before us, reaching a space humanity may enter soon enough, and so they speak from a place we have not yet learned to find a voice for.[21]

That call, all those beautiful harmonics of the family singing out in the night, that call gives us an answer to the question we confront when we stand face-to-face with dismembered kin. Someone, perhaps it was god, is before us in the tree, and on the ground. Someone has soaked into the Earth, and is rattled by winter winds. Someone is tacked up above the coco-pops, someone is being used as home décor. These bodies call us not only with their faces, and not ever with abstracted faces or with face as metaphor. They call to us with their defenseless flesh, with their skin, and their blood, and the little white socks.

We are witnesses, and as we probe the ethics of relation and substance, perhaps working our way toward the uncertainty of a quantum god, we may yet engage with the wider gravity of keeping faith in the midst of devastation.

10. World-Crazy

My Aboriginal teachers taught me to experience a world of uncertainty—a world of shape-shifting and flux, where much that exists may be something other than it appears. Old Tim Yilngayarri told strange and funny stories that led me to understand that the power of being clever inheres in otherwise ordinary beings, enabling them to do things that ordinary beings cannot do. The very concept of cleverness thus acknowledges that ordinary life has its limits, and also asserts that some creatures are capable of exceeding those limits. One of my favorite stories is about Old Riley, a man who died long before I had a chance to meet him. Once when he was away from home, traveling the country, he killed a cow because he needed the meat. At some point he realized that the police were after him, and knowing that people were jailed for years for cattle killing, he turned himself into a bird. He became a chicken hawk, to be precise, and flew home to his own country. Knowing such stories, you have to ask: this bird that you see—is it a bird, or is it a man?

Extra-ordinary powers such as those of the Old Riley story strain my comprehension, but even ordinariness, as Aboriginal people experience it, might seem extra-ordinary from the perspective of mainstream Western science. Living beings, including country itself, are alert to what is happening in the world, are watching what is going on and seeking to understand the nature of the webs of events which they observe and in which they are observed. I learned these lessons interactively. There was, for example, the daily drama with my pet cockatoo. Often my neighbors and I sat at the fire after breakfast, chatting and watching the world in its eventfulness. Every morning my cockatoo would fly off to try to join the bush cockatoos, and every morning when he landed in a tree with them they would all take flight, leaving him there alone. My heart went out to the young cockatoo who had been captured and was now trying to make a place for himself in the world from which he had been taken. My neighbors took a more analytic approach, wondering why the others always flew away. At last they said that they thought the bush birds must have heard cocky speaking English and concluded that he must be clever.[1]

Cleverness is dispersed across species, for not only might a bird be a person, it could equally be a clever bird. One would understand what one was encountering by remaining alert to actions and consequences. To live in a world of such uncertainty requires the understanding that humans are not the only sentient beings on Earth. It therefore requires immense knowledge of the others, knowledge that enables one to know what is ordinary and what is extra-ordinary, not only for humans but for every living thing. Furthermore, it requires continuing attentiveness, and people were asking questions all the time: What was that? What is happening? If forms are not fixed and if intentional action is widespread, then understanding must look to actions and events, searching for patterns and positing possible connections. Clever people have an important epistemological role in a system in which mutability is always a possibility. Along with those who are very old and very wise, they understand patterns and deviations from patterns. They know what constitutes ordinariness and what is out of the ordinary. Furthermore, they understand that the nature of life on Earth includes both pattern and deviation, fixity and mutability, the orderly and the unexpected.

Time travel isn't hard, but it does take imagination. Let's go to Paris in the year 1936. A spark of Earth intellectual excitement has just flared up—the existential philosopher Lev Shestov has read the new book by the anthropologist Lucien Lévy-Bruhl, and has become passionately excited by tribal people's experience of a world of metamorphosis and uncertainty. Lévy-Bruhl put forward a case for an embodied experience of a wider reality (relative to that defined by Western science), and Shestov welcomed this account. In a number of brilliant essays, Shestov had argued for the significance of the body, of birth, of time, indeed, of all the experiential life of the living world in its transience and mutability.

Shestov, the Russian émigré, and Lévy-Bruhl, the Parisian academic, were born within a decade of each other, and both died shortly before World War II. Both men would have come under Nazi rule if they had remained in occupied Paris, and both would probably have died in concentration camps. Lévy-Bruhl was born in

Paris in 1857. He studied ethics and then gravitated to anthropology and the study of "primitive" humanity, as tribal peoples were then labeled, becoming one of the founders of the Institute of Ethnology at the Sorbonne. He was one of the great "armchair anthropologists," and, along with Sir James Frazer and others, he worked with ideas about the evolution of culture, influenced by Darwin's theories of the evolution of species. Lévy-Bruhl's thinking took a turn late in life, changing from an evolutionary framework to something more radical.[2] As we will see, it was the radical edge of his thought that so excited Shestov.

Lévy-Bruhl was fascinated by the kind of thought he classed as "primitive" and that he encountered in studying the work of field anthropologists. He contends that tribal people's experience of nature is fluid, and that they experience the power of creation as a process of flux and metamorphosis. "Neither living beings nor objects are monomorphic," and "the extraordinary is part of what happens normally," he writes.[3] In contrast to some of the experts on whose work he draws, Lévy-Bruhl does not propose that natives have inferior mental skills. He really wants to understand different ways of thinking, and in trying to communicate his understanding he describes what we might now call a poetics of sentient nature: "Their metaphysics is quite spontaneous; it is the result of the frequent, one might say constant, experience of a reality which goes beyond and dominates all common nature, and yet is present and active in it at all times."[4] Lévy-Bruhl uses the term "pre-logical" to define a type of thought that he was struggling to understand. He no longer wanted the prefix "pre" to be set in an evolutionary sequence; rather he wanted to indicate another kind of logic based on different principles. Most particularly, he wanted to describe a kind of logic that does not put an argument against contradiction in center stage.[5] In today's language, we would say that he is aiming to describe the logic of "both-and," the logic of connection rather than exclusion, of difference organized into relationships. He calls this logic the "Law of Participation."[6] David Abram describes it eloquently: "Lévy-Bruhl used the word 'participation' to characterize the animistic logic of indigenous, oral peoples—for whom ostensibly 'inanimate' objects like stone or mountains are often thought to be alive, for whom certain names, spoken aloud, may be felt to influence at a distance the things or beings that they name, for whom particular plants, particular animals, particular places and persons and powers may all be felt to *participate* in one another's existence, influencing each other and being influenced in turn."[7]

Shestov's 1936 essay about Lévy-Bruhl's *La mythologie primitive* is a work of heady enthusiasm. He was particularly excited by the fact that Lévy-Bruhl was daring enough to propose that Western philosophy could gain critical perspectives on itself by engaging with tribal thought: "The study of the spiritual world of primitive man pushed him to a still more difficult and serious question: . . . Are we not obliged to test our own ideas about what truth is by that which we learn from" these tribal peoples?[8] In asking this question, Shestov turned on its head a cherished Western history that put Western people at the apex of human achievement. Rather than positing the "primitive" as a distant ancestor, Shestov and Lévy-Bruhl were seeking dialogue. Their search was predicated on the idea that learning can go in multiple directions and that the insights of others may help us perceive, and perhaps overcome, some of the limitations of our own thought. There is a temptation here, often labeled Romanticism, that would see others as having insights that civilisation has occluded for us. According to the Romantic vision, the primitive, like the child, has a clearer vision of reality than does the civilized person or the adult. As I understand Shestov and Lévy-Bruhl, neither of them was buying into dichotomized, Romanticized thinking. Shestov's question was pertinent to his ongoing critique of modernity, and he welcomed the idea that the narrowness of modernity's thought can be enlarged by engaging with the thinking of people who are outside the modernity of the West. Lévy-Bruhl repudiated his either-or views on primitive versus modern thinking, suggesting that differences in thought are better explained by pattern, emphasis and context. Perhaps he was learning to think inclusively (like a "primitive").

In any event, the expanded reality Lévy-Bruhl describes is the flint against which Shestov's most cherished ideas spark, for Shestov was a passionate advocate of a kind of "craziness," by which he meant a person's immersion in the specific, situated, fully sensed, and fully committed life in the living world of birth and death. Shestov's craziness is a commitment to transience, flux, and uncertainty, and may well seem mad if one is deeply attached to that which is deemed to be eternal and immutable. His argument with the dominant Western philosophical tradition was precisely over this point: its attachment to that which it posits as eternal and immutable denigrates all the transient life of the real world.

Imagine Shestov and Lévy-Bruhl sitting around the campfire with Old Tim. The clever man might have wondered what all the fuss was about, since the worldview they found so exotic was the mode of reality in which he was thoroughly at home. Let us join the two Parisians around the fire. In order to facilitate an enlarged conversation, let us welcome Nobel laureate Ilya Prigogine, and three great feminist thinkers—Donna Haraway, Freya Mathews, and Val Plumwood. Where Donna goes, Cayenne goes too, so there will be a cross-cultural meeting among the dogs as well as among the humans. This group of thinkers is not likely to converse for long without finding some good points for disagreement, but my interest is in how together they further our understandings of uncertainty, life, love, death, and ethics.

Old Tim's stories always involved humor, and he will have gotten everyone laughing. One of his favorites was about the time he grappled with a Rainbow Snake and saved the life of a White man. We'll interrupt the story and ask Tim to tell us what a Rainbow Snake is, and he'll explain that it's an extremely powerful snake who lives in the waterholes that have permanent water, and is the "boss" for rain. He'll tell us that once when he was much younger he saw a white man floundering; he dived into the river, wrestled with the Rainbow, got the guy out of its whirlpool grip, pulled him up on the bank of the river, drained the water out of him, made fires to warm him, and waited with him until he came around. When the White man opened his eyes and shook his head, disoriented and completely bewildered, there was Tim gazing at him across one of the fires. The guy asked, in what might have been some of the most sincere words ever to pass between a White man and an Aboriginal man in those days, "What happened?"

After all this Rainbow Snake wrestling, and all these good life-saving techniques, there they were: Tim on one side of the fire, the sodden White man on the other. All the guy wanted was to know what happened, and when Old Tim got to this part of the story he started laughing in advance of the punch line. His answer was: "I don't know!" And every time he told the story, he laughed all over again.

Tim's story is inevitably situated within the context of colonization, and it is not hard to imagine that he enjoyed the power of refusing a White person's demand. At the same time, there is more to be considered. I asked Tim why he didn't just tell the guy what had happened, and he said that that is not the way it is done. His enigmatic non-answer to me was certainly a way of dealing with a naïve anthropologist, but perhaps it wouldn't matter who was asking the questions. Saving a person's life is one thing; purporting to know what happened is quite another thing. Why did the Rainbow grab this particular guy? What led to this event? Why was Old Tim there at the right time to wrestle him out of the river? And what would the man do with the life that had so unexpectedly been restored to him? More expansively: Why do some people die while others live? How is it that life is plucked out of death? The story of this event went way beyond anything Old Tim would claim to understand. Perhaps it is exactly that limit—that recognition of how the eventfulness of the living world exceeds our capacity to claim to know—that brought Tim into laughter and delight. Of course the expression on the guy's face must have been funny, but there was also the enormity of the question, the obtuse demand to have the unknowable explained. For a clever person like Old Tim, a holy fool in the true sense of the term, the question was absurd, and he gave a truthful and appropriately absurd response.

Ilya Prigogine knows a thing or two about limits. He tells us that his work has always attracted hostility. When he was a young man, he "wrestled" with one of the senior scientists in his field. He presented a conference paper in 1946 on irreversible thermodynamics, and the "greatest expert in the field of thermodynamics" said of him, "I am astonished that this young man is so interested in nonequilibrium physics. Irreversible processes are transient, why not wait and study equilibrium as everyone else does?" Prigogine was speechless. Perhaps if he had known Old Tim, he would have had the presence of mind to respond with appropriate absurdity, "I don't know." In fact, much later he offered a response that was a restrained but passionate defense of the real: "But we are all transient. Is it not natural to be interested in our common human condition?"[9] Part of what makes our common Earth condition so interesting is that that which may yet be is infinitely more extravagant than that which already has been. In scientific terms, indeterminacy breaks time symmetry (see chapter 4), and therefore "the possible is richer than the real."[10]

Like Shestov, Prigogine contrasts this understanding with Plato's thought. Plato linked truth to being and thus to an "unchanging reality beyond becoming."[11] The beauty, one might say, of immutability is that it is totally certain, totally predictable. Prigogine's work is focused on uncertainty. He writes at the cusp of major changes in Western thought, and speaks in defense of uncertainty. A further effect of uncertainty is that knowledge is never complete, total knowing is not possible, and the possibilities of the living world always are greater than the mind or knowledge system that wants to understand.

The Australian philosopher Val Plumwood has been sitting here quietly, but now she has to intervene. She has written extremely eloquently about Plato, death, and modernity, and she wants to make the connection between death and certainty, and to turn the conversation toward the fact that Western thought is having great difficulty finding a life-affirming account of death. Plumwood understands Plato to have been working toward an account of life that would sustain immortality in the face of death. He worked with a soul-body dualism that aligned the soul with that which is immortal and unchanging, and aligned the body with the changing, dying world of nature. He then could argue that the human task is to rise above nature. Plato arrived at an otherworld identity that claimed to cancel death. In Plumwood's words: "Platonic philosophy . . . not only devalues nature, it is profoundly anti-ecological and anti-life."[12] From Plato and on into Christianity the same idea continued: the meaning of life is elsewhere—among the stars, or in heaven; the real self is the soul, and the world of transience and death is to be transcended.

Plumwood goes on to point out that secular modernity impacted on the Christian and Platonic worldviews by denying the existence of another world, or a resurrection of the soul in heaven. It abolished that which claimed to redeem or make sense of both life and death, and it offered nothing in its place. In fact, she argues in detail that modernity has proved incapable of offering a life-affirming account of death.[13]

Val's talk about death has got everybody worked up, and Old Tim is keen to tell about his father's death. His wife, Mary Rutungali, joins the circle and shares the story:

Tim: They put him in the grave, I'll tell you. You know that big hole? That big hole right by the store, the Katherine store? You've seen it?

Debbie: Yeah.

Tim: That's the grave of my old man.

Debbie: Oh, true?

Tim: And he got up, he got up Rainbow then.

Debbie: He got up Rainbow?

Mary: Yeah. Got up.

Tim: That's my daddy at Darwin then, alive.

Mary: He was there then.

Tim: He was there at Darwin, with the buffalo shooters, at Marrakai [Station]. I've been there. My old man was still alive. He was dead there [at Katherine], and that thing came out, that Rainbow, and he flew up. He was there really, going to Darwin. You know my old man too fucking too clever. Really clever. . . . He went over to Marrakai, and stayed around there, at Marrakai. I went out from here. My old man came to Bagot [Aboriginal reserve in Darwin]. . . . He took me to Marrakai, with the buffalo shooters. . . . My mother came, all my brothers, they came to see him. And mother went and cried over him. Old man cried over me. Finish.[14]

I am listening to how Old Tim's story tells us that death is a metamorphic event, a transition from life to life. Not everyone who dies is "too fucking too clever"; not everyone "gets up Rainbow," but Tim's account of his father's death is consistent with every death story I heard from Aboriginal people in this region. When a person dies, one part of their life continues on in the world.

Stories like this can make a person shiver, and we move closer to the fire. As we do so, we see that Shestov is becoming wild with excitement. This is a poetics in which the event of death is turned back toward life; death and life are partners in a metamorphic flow of comings and goings, turning and returning across zones of birthing and dying. Shestov is excited by the "answer" Old Tim's story can be heard to offer to the Western issue of nothingness against which Shestov wrote passionately. For existentialists such as Shestov (whether religious or not), the question of nothingness loomed large. Now he is hearing a story that keeps death here on Earth, that treats death as metamorphosis and holds it in dialogue with life. This is an Earth-focused account of both birth and death. People have histories that precede their birth, and while death inevitably entails grief and loss, there is no nothingness. Shestov is wondering how this liminal zone ought properly to be characterized; certainly it is not the chasm of emptiness posited by nihilist thought.

Before Shestov can launch into another critique of modernity, Cayenne starts barking in her cheerful way. Probably she has sensed that Donna is getting fidgety. Haraway and Cayenne have done serious work and play together in agility training, entering together and encountering each other in "the contact zone." Donna reworks Heidegger's term "the Open" to enable it to do the work that is needed here. For Heidegger, the Open is the place of encounter where a human being is freed from all the attachments and all the sense of the significance of the living world, and comes face-to-face with the nothingness that gives rise to Being. Within this space Heidegger proposes that humans have access to others, although it is unclear how this could happen. Haraway notes that Heidegger is searching for encounter unencumbered with the instrumentality of technological use. The cost is "profound boredom."[15] In contrast to Heidegger, Haraway proposes the Open as a site where encounter with another, in her case an animal other, produces a shock of communicative understanding: "*This* and *here* are who and what we are."[16] We might think of the open as a zone, or we might think of it as a process. Haraway uses the term "contact zone" in her seriously playful study of humans and animals. She works with the understanding that the world is contingent and open-ended, that we and other living and nonliving things engage in world making. Our interactions are constitutive both of who we are and of what possibilities for world making, or unmaking, are opened up through our actions.

I share Shestov's reservations about nothingness, and like numerous other scholars I am fond of pointing out that humans can only be thought to arise out of nothingness if one accepts that the whole of the cosmos including the whole of the living world, is "nothing." That old mind/matter dualism causes so much grief. But Haraway's point is not to argue for specific terms; rather she argues for world making that affirms and enhances life in connectivity and without hierarchy.

Shestov made the point again and again that our understanding of our real place in the real world was seriously damaged by our commitment to Certainty. He spoke of "death" or "killing" in this context, of "killing" the "living will" within one's self and renouncing one's own personality.[17] Here we may think of a kind of moral death in which the possibility of a loving, ethical engagement with the living world is killed through the denigration of transience. So here, too, is the death of ethics (as we saw in another context in chapter 3), for if the transient, situated, idiosyncratic self is suppressed, who or what is left to participate in dramas of encounter and recognition? His excitement with native people's acquaintance with metamorphosis arose out of his awareness of damage and seemed to offer a way back into connectivity.

The Australian philosopher Freya Mathews wants to push this idea a bit more. She uses the term "de-realization" to describe the West's catastrophic plunge into denigration of the real. De-realisation results from the West's mind/matter dualism, which ascribes mind to human subjectivity, and leaves matter in a state of mindlessness. She shows the terrifying implication of this dualism—that it leaves no ground for epistemological connectivity with the living world.[18] Donna is nodding in agreement here, as is Val. Feminist scholars have developed an insightful critique of dualisms that works across gender, nature/culture and mind/matter, and that encompasses philosophy and action. Haraway has pointed out that this mind/matter dualism "should have withered long ago in the light of feminist and many other criticisms, but the fantastic mind/body binary has proved remarkably resilient."[19]

To turn away from dualisms is to turn toward life in its complexity and connectivity. Mathews shows us that such a turn brings us directly into a domain of both eros and ethics. She works with two main characteristics of life: its desire for its own becoming (*conatus*), and its desire for connectivity (*orexis*). Each desire is implicated in the other: life wants to live, and life wants to live (indeed, must live) with others.[20] In one sense, the desire for connectivity is a statement of the ecological fact that organisms and environments permeate each other, are mutually constitutive, and thus mutually necessary and sustaining. A stronger statement involves synergy. If life is always more than the sum of its parts, then living beings and groups of living beings are parts of broader domains of connectivity in which they find their own becoming in time. Life's desire for its own becoming is achieved through interactions of living and non-living matter. Life's desire therefore involves both eros and ethics. Eros is the desire—for life, for connection, for others, and for self. Ethics open us to interactive, world-making dramas of encounter that facilitate the capacity to live together in the long term.

Shestov is happy to be pushed, and delighted to push back. When he urged us to break out of Certainty, he knew we would break into specificity. His call for love in the midst of transient multiplicities prompts Shestov to call us into "God-craziness." His vision for humanity is that we have the freedom to act on faith, and while keeping faith with uncertainty may look and feel like craziness to those who are accustomed to value Certainty, Shestov argues that this is the appropriate response to God and the world.[21] He urges us to make a turn toward Earth. Against the eternal, he offers us time. Against immutability, he urges us to love the world in its flux, and thus he calls us to find ourselves crazy and in love with the world of life.

Dear Shestov, I am saying, I would love to join you in craziness, but I'm not too keen on "God." May we not respond to your call by joining in the craziness and mystery of Earth? In my vision of turning toward Earth, we engage in dramas of encounter and recognition, becoming "crazy with" others as well as "crazy for" others. I imagine world-craziness as a strong call for us to cherish birth and growth, and to love that which is perilous. The others we will become crazy with are here with us; they/we are Earth others in relation to each other. World-craziness immerses us in the power, resilience, connectivity, and uncertainty of the living Earth.

11. Solomon's Wisdom

Colin Thubron, traveler and writer, tells a strange story about "King Solomon's tomb" in Central Asia. In Kyrgyzstan, near a town called Osh, he visited a place about which he reports, "Some say that Solomon was murdered here, and that his black dogs still lurk in the fissures of the rocks, where they lapped his blood and ate his body." Those fissures, the homes of the dogs, were believed in times past to have a healing power, and invalids would press their heads into the crevices as a cure.[1]

This story gave me shivers. Many people experience horror at the thought of being eaten; Val Plumwood's account of being taken by a crocodile explores some of the phenomenological and ethical dimensions of discovering one's self to be prey.[2] Perhaps especially because dogs are such devoted companions, the thought of becoming their food seems to many of us especially awful. And then there are the curses. Psalm 63, for example, includes this curse on one's enemies:

> May those who seek to destroy my life
> > Enter the depths of the earth.
> May they be gutted by the sword;
> > May they be prey to jackals.

Similarly John Dominic Crossan, in his essay "The Dogs beneath the Cross," writes that the shame and pain of crucifixion is located not only in the public and exceedingly painful death, but also in the withholding of a proper burial. The dying person would know that his body would be eaten by scavengers, including dogs, and that his relatives would suffer yet another grief because they would not be allowed to give the body a proper burial.[3] In more recent times, reports coming from the city of Falluja in Iraq during the U.S. war emphasized the horror and magnitude of death by linking dogs and the dead. Ali Fadhil visited Falluja and wrote that the town was devastated: "The bodies, some of them civilians and some of them

insurgents, were still rotting inside. There were dead dogs everywhere, lying in the middle of the streets." He goes on to say, "The
Baghdad Hospital for Infectious Diseases admits one case of rabies
every week. The problem is that infected dogs are eating the corpses
and spreading the disease."[4] These images connect dogs and death
in a realm of terror and dishonor, such that the dogs amplify the
grief and horror surrounding unburied corpses.

But might King Solomon's black dogs tell a different story? The
descendants of those dogs still guard the tomb, healing powers remain, and thus loyalty, continuity, and the power of life are located
here. What if the story gestures toward a relationship of love and
loyalty that includes death? What if death is turned back toward life
through the work of one's companions and protectors?

In the legend of Solomon, his tomb, and his dogs, we get a glim-
mer of a domain in which love, death, wisdom, and nature belong
together and affirm continuities of life across the zone of death. Let
us enter this domain through the most beautiful book of the Bible—
the Song of Songs, which is Solomon's. This book was probably
written down about the third century BCE. There is nothing to suggest that Solomon was the author, or even that it had a single author.
Solomon figures in the poem primarily as a "central figure in the
lovers' fantasies."[5] Still, it seems appropriate to attribute the Song
to Solomon. According to tradition, he was a lover of nature: his
ring enabled him to understand the languages of animals. And he
was the great king with a thousand women (wives and concubines),
a lover of women (and political alliances). Most spectacularly, perhaps, he was known for his wisdom. The Song of Songs concerns
love, wisdom, and close interactions between humans and nature,
all qualities of the legendary Solomon.

The Song offers wisdom that is radically different to the standard
view of ancient wisdom literature. A specialist in this literature defines it as "the reasoned search for specific ways to ensure personal
well-being in everyday life, to make sense of extreme adversity and
vexing anomalies, and to transmit this hard-earned knowledge so
that successive generations will embody it."[6] On this view, wisdom
suggests the means for achieving a satisfying but perhaps boring life.
Job sits ambiguously in this tradition since the friends who appear
to offer wisdom are chastised by God. In contrast, the Song offers a

wild and passionate wisdom that is situated in the ongoing here and now of the living world.

The beautiful translation by Ariel and Chana Bloch brings the Song of Songs elegantly to life. As they describe the poem, the Song is not so much a story as a series of episodes "about the sexual awakening of a young woman and her lover." It is set in spring, the Earth is coming alive after winter, and the lovers partake of the joy of earth's bursting forth as they discover each other in their youth and passion.[7] The Song of Songs revels both in the glories of eros and in the glories of Earth. It is thus unique within the Bible, as many authors note. Robert Alter, for example, discusses the contrast between the Song and the rest of the Bible by noting what is *not* in the Song of Songs—no moral conflict, no nationhood or destiny, no "looming" theology.[8]

The poem speaks in the voices of the lovers, but it does not construct a human-centric vision. Bloch and Bloch suggest that elsewhere in the Bible nature is the mirror of God, and the preeminence of God mirrors a preeminence of humans on Earth. They further suggest that the idea of human preeminence may have been formed "in reaction to the neighboring pagan cultures with their animal gods." In the Song of Songs, by contrast, "the name of God does not even appear, and there is no opposition between human and animal, no hierarchy, no dominion." Indeed, Bloch and Bloch go on to suggest that divinity lives within the lovers and Earth.[9] Here we encounter a Wild God in full flower, an erotic dogsology dedicated to the power of the dance of desire. Shestov's God-crazy passion and my world-crazy passion converge in their encounter with the Song of Songs, finding here a place where they can settle together happily, even joyfully.

Eros pervades the whole of the Song, and the exuberant power of sensual connection arises again and again. Sensuous, empathetic modes of touch, scent, vision, taste, and sound, join with emotional, passionate desires for merging, mingling, departing, and returning. Such sensuous connections speak to a theory of self—an erotic self—that is always seeking connection.[10] Robert Alter's afterword to the Blochs' translation is a brief essay on the metaphysics of love. He writes of an erotics of commingling, fluidity, and porosity wherein humans and the wider world flow into and through each other.[11] This vision of love parallels current philosophical work on ecological erotics. It works toward an erotics that is of, within, and for this Earth, and of, within, and for Earth creatures. The fact that we humans approach an ecological erotics through our own human experience does not make erotics human-centric. Rather, it acknowledges that a sensuous engagement with life on Earth is achieved through the body, and the human being inhabits a human body. An ecological erotics that generously celebrates connection has to start with the body that is given, and each start is a fresh venture into the erotics of encounter and return.

Freya Mathews has introduced eros into ecology and ethics through her work with the living organism's twin desires—to sustain itself (*conatus*) and to engage with others beyond the self (*orexis*). The longing *for* others, the longing to reach out and to touch, can be understood as a call *to* others. In the ongoing recursive connectivities of the living world, every living thing is being called and is calling, is coming into encounter, and thus is always coming. Always coming to others, always coming with others, always longing for connection and always pulling back. This is life's eros—to reach out for others, to turn toward self, to turn toward others. The longing and the touch bring self and other into mutuality. Mathews writes, "And to the extent that the self achieves this connection, it will experience the energization, the brimming sense of plenitudinousness, that accrues from feeling fully alive."[12]

Unlike other books of the Bible, most of the created world is brought into the Song of Songs. Plants and animals, in particular, become vivid metaphors:

> Like a lily in a field
> Of thistles,
> Such is my love
> among the young women.[13]

The imagery is given such full and free play that the boundary between figure and referent becomes quite fluid, as Alter discusses in his superb essay "The Garden of Metaphor." He offers as one example the passage 2:8–10 in which the lover is likened to a stag (italics indicate that the words are being spoken by the young woman):

The voice of my love: listen!
Bounding over the mountains
Toward me, across the hills.

My love is a gazelle, a wild stag.
There he stands on the other side
Of our wall, gazing
Between the stones.

And he calls to me:
Hurry, my love, my friend,
And come away!

Alter writes that the figure becomes *both* stag *and* lover with the consequence that "the lover is entirely assimilated into the natural world at the same time that the natural world is felt to be profoundly in consonance with the lovers."[14] This fluidity between humans and other living things is enhanced by the pacing of motion and encounter. The first words give us the breathless rush of love and life: "Kiss me, make me drunk with your kisses!" The wider world is equally invoked in flow and flux: seasons, and the coming forth, growing, and ripening of plants and animals in various stages of maturity, flowing water, rising winds, desert dust, budding flowers, and the fragrance that wafts from them in the evening air, beautiful fragrances that mingle with the lovers, the flowers, the gentle night air, and the body's passion.

There is motion, there is fluid metamorphosis between nature and humans, and there are the voices that call out. "Hurry, my love, my friend / And come away!" They call to each other, and they call up the world around them:

Awake, north wind! O south wind, come,
breathe upon my garden,
let its spices stream out.
Let my lover come into his garden
and taste its delicious fruit.[15]

There is communication here too—often conveyed through senses other than vision. The fragrance of flowers, for example, announces their presence in the darkness of night. The wind picks up the glorious odors and carries them along, linking them to the lovers. So the young woman speaks of her fragrance waking the night; she and the flowers, the darkness, the breeze, the announcement and the attraction all merge. Similarly, the lovers speak of going to see the new green by the brook, and she has said that "wherever we lie our bed is green."[16] As human eros is charged up with passion it mingles with the Earth. Before long every reference to Earth is a reference also to passion, and so an ecological erotics is sung up. One can never again imagine hills or cinnamon without imagining hills covered with cinnamon, lovers in passion, animals bounding across spices, and life dazzling itself with its own abundant beauty and desire.

Most scholars take the relationship between life and death to be the core metaphysical message of the Song. The relevant verse proclaims the equivalent strengths of love and death—"for love is fierce as death," or in other translations, "as strong as death."[17] The words are explicit, and yet the significance of equivalence may remain problematic. In an essay on allegory and the Song of Songs, William Phipps talks about all the effort that early Christians put into allegories that would make the Song of Songs palatable within a philosophical context that valued soul over and above body, mind over matter, reason over emotion, and other great dualisms. His main point is that this process of allegorization involved turning the meaning of the poem into its opposite. His prime example is carnal passion, which was transposed into a more acceptable discarnate spirituality. It is a fascinating essay, made weird by the fact that Phipps concludes by performing exactly the kind of transposition that implicitly he is rejecting. He writes, "The affirmation 'Love is as strong as death' is excelled only by the New Testament proclamation that love is even stronger than death."[18] In Phipps's heavy gesture, this beautiful passage becomes a foreshadowing of a greater truth, revealed in the New Testament, that love and death are *not* equivalent, but rather that love transcends death. In short, the passage is taken typologically to foreshadow something quite different to what it says. The difference between the two statements really matters. The Song works with an equivalence that plays itself out in Earthly life, and it shows how equivalence is sustained. Phipps's move pulls the meaning of love and death out of this world, and out of ecological erotics, locating meaning in the kind of transcendent postdeath theology that Plumwood has analyzed so succinctly (see chapter 10).

We would not expect the Song of Songs to say a lot about death, the grave, and the afterlife (Sheol), but of course the Bible as a whole has precious little to say about the afterlife, and the afterlife is something of a hidden secret in the Bible, as we have seen. And yet, in biblical times, as in preceding millennia, humans lived within communities that included the dead as well as living.[19]

As discussed in chapter 7, the archaeologist Rachel Hallote demonstrates that the Bible disguises how people in its era perceived death. Archaeology shows the existence of a death cult that persisted for millennia and that was widespread across the region before, during, and after the biblical era (defined in approximate terms as 700 BCE–AD 70). According to Tal, "burial complexes . . . were . . . used by all the inhabitants of Palestine without faith differentiation . . . from the tombs of Iron Age Palestine [to] . . . the Roman period."[20] Similarly, Block-Smith's research into burials from the Iron Age through to the early historical period shows that the cult of the dead flourished in spite of an "official" policy to "discredit the dead":

> [The cult of the dead] was integrated into Judahite social, religious and economic fabric. The lack of change . . . in the material remains uncovered through archaeological fieldwork, including in Jerusalem, supports the interpretation that there was no general shift in practices or attitudes regarding the dead. If common practice is to be labelled "popular" then Jerusalem residents including Judahite national and religious authorities also followed "popular" practice. The divine ancestors continued as vital entities in Judahite religion and society as long as the kingdom existed, flourishing in defiance of "official" dicta against it.[21]

In sum, the boundary between the living and the dead was porous in the extreme. The existence of this popular culture was suppressed in the Bible; we glimpse it primarily through injunctions against it. Archaeological evidence tells what the Bible conceals: the living and the dead were partners in the ongoing project of life.

Death practices in the ancient world connected life and death in the popular context of death feasts. Marvin Pope discusses such feasts in vivid detail, drawing on ancient texts from nearby regions, and describing events in which the participants revel in drunkenness and wild, unregulated sex. Death and sex were bound together in magnificent excess as people disported themselves in "love feasts" that responded to death through the assertion of life.[22] According to Pope, the drinking house, such as is mentioned in the Song of Songs, was "a place in which banquets were held in both mourning and revelry for the dead, with drunkenness and sacral sexual intercourse."[23] Ugaritic texts describe the gods "reeling in drunken delirium, wallowing in excrement and urine, and collapsing as if dead."[24] Isaiah 28:7–8 warns against such excesses, as did other prophets of the Old Testament, and, later, the early Christian church Fathers.[25]

Iconography of death feasts shows the mourner-celebrants on their couches, and under the couch was a dog.[26] Speculation about the role of the dog ranges from the delightfully homey to the bizarre; I don't presume to offer an explanation for the past, but one gets the point that if banquet halls became fouled with vomit (and worse), it would be handy to have dogs to clean up the mess. More significantly, though, the iconography can be taken to indicate the beautiful complexity of dogs' vigorous involvement in both death and sex. The complexity of dogs offers insight into our own complexity, and into the complexity of Earth life more generally.

The Bible asserts that dogs are unclean and must be kept at a distance. It is impossible to know when this attitude came into being, but we can state with certainty that it had not always been thus. The first evidence in the world of companion burial comes from the area that is now Israel. Eleven or twelve thousand years ago, long before the biblical era, an elderly person was buried with their hand resting on a puppy.[27] The most astounding discovery dating to the biblical period is the massive dog cemetery in the region at Ashkelon. Here, excavations dated to around 500 BCE reveal the skeletons of more than one thousand dogs, each carefully placed on its side in its grave with its tail curving toward its feet.[28] It is not yet known how the dog cemetery relates to biblical concepts of dogs and death, but it certainly complicates the idea that dogs were to be shunned. The biblical scholar Alan Cadwallader has pointed out to me that this cemetery is pressing biblical scholars to rethink verse 23:18 in Deuteronomy, which makes reference to the price of a dog, as it now seems possible that the verse is alluding to ritual matters that suggest relationships of respect. We can imagine that as with death and death cults, so with dogs: the Bible's silence is not evidence of absence, but rather absence of evidence—an elision of stories that were not consistent with the Yahwist religion that was being put forward.

Just as an insistence on human preeminence and the erasure of death cults differentiated Israelites from their "pagan" neighbors, so too with dogs. The Israelite people were surrounded by other peoples for whom dogs were valued and beloved companions. Philippe Erikson discusses pets in ancient Greece and Rome and concludes that across a broad region and through many centuries before and after the time of Christ, there were dog burials, epitaphs, tombstones. Dogs were praised for their loyalty, bravery, and similar features, and above all for the pleasure they provided their people—their affection, their playfulness. Special pets were termed "foster child," as one beautiful epitaph demonstrates: "To Helena, foster child, soul without comparison and deserving of praise."[29]

Similarly, the Zoroastrian Persians kept dogs as pets, and gave them special offerings of food because of their powerful connection with the spirit world. Dogs were held to have a moral character, and to experience death in much the same way as humans.[30] Egyptians, too, kept dogs as pets, naming them and incorporating them into families. Some dogs were taken through into the afterlife in mummified form, and were placed in family crypts. Egyptian dogs' names are delightful because they are perfectly comprehensible to us today. They included: Brave One, Reliable, Good Herdsman, Antelope, and even Useless.[31]

Not only were the neighbors of the Hebrew peoples fond of dogs, they were peoples for whom the transition from life, through death, and into the afterlife was mediated by dogs. One need only think of Anubis, the dog or dog-headed Egyptian being that supervised the embalming and burial of the deceased and who guided the dead to the underworld. The dog at the threshold of life and death is a compelling image: Hecate, goddess of crossroads with her companion dogs who call out when a person is born and when a person dies;

Cerberus, the three-headed guardian of Hades; Yama's four-eyed dogs. According to one scholar, "dogs appear as guides for the soul in Indic and Iranian traditions, as guards of the afterworld in Greek, Roman, Germanic and Celtic traditions, and as choosers of the dead or messenger of death in Indic and Celtic traditions."[32] Many more examples from other parts of the world could be cited, including Anubis, of course, the Popul Vuh of Mayans, and never neglecting Old Tim's stories of the Dingo and the Moon.

Returning to the Middle East, the connection between dogs and death was particularly intimate among Zoroastrians. Recall that Solomon's dogs are said to guard the tomb, and that they ate his flesh and drank his blood. It takes Zoroastrianism to bring a wild wisdom to this account. The great scholar Mary Boyce has summarized Zoroastrian relationships with dogs; she holds that in Zoroastrian thought, a dead body is held to be contaminating, and so it would be an insult to Earth to bury the body. Corpses are exposed to be fed on by animals. Dogs devoured the contaminating flesh of corpses, and as they were not themselves contaminated by it they were held in high regard. Furthermore, the spirit of a dead person had to cross a bridge of judgment, and dogs were there to help.[33] A further point of significance between dogs and the dead was that food given ritually to a dog would reach the departed soul.[34]

As the intriguing new evidence from the excavations at Ashkelon suggests, relationships between humans, dogs, and death may be another hidden secret within the Bible. It may be that when Solomon's dogs ate his body they were giving him a respectful farewell in a faraway land, and that in their loyal way they have stayed with his tomb ever since.

The connection between dogs and sex is both more obvious and more complicated than the dog/death nexus. Dogs do not respect rules for sex, and one idea about the role of dogs beneath the couch at death feasts is the speculation that dogs were meant to knock over the torches, plunging the place into darkness so that in their drunken revels people might have sex with their own close, and otherwise forbidden, kin. Apparently it is for this reason that Tertullian refers to dogs as "the pimps of darkness."[35]

Not only are dogs totally promiscuous, they are also so energetic that they become stuck together. Old Tim, the dog man with the most wonderful earthiness, had a lot of laughs over this. Dingoes are our ancestors, in Tim's stories, and so our ancestors got stuck too. Tim's story starts with an erotic gaze. He tells of a time when women and men first started looking at each other with blood in their eyes:

> There was a big mob of women, and men were saying, "Ah, that good lady, oooh, that good woman!" And the women were looking around for boyfriends, and they saw men and they reckoned: "Oh, good! We want them! We want them for married" [Tim's pleasant euphemism for sex]. Before, men and women were getting naughty [another euphemism] and didn't stop for three or four years. Everybody was like that. They couldn't come off [each other]. Women wouldn't come back [from their rendezvous]; they'd be stuck for two, three, four hours. That's what we were doing. And the Dreaming doctor said, "No." He fixed them up, making them human. People said, "Ah, the way we are now, we can be boyfriend and girlfriend, and we'll do it the right way."

Old Tim explained that this is the public version of a story that has more detail when told within men's secret domain. With all the storytelling talents at his disposal, he made the story as vivid as possible, using hand signs to indicate the parts of the body being discussed, and allusive terms to speak to some parts of the story, and laughing from time to time as he gestured or demonstrated the hungry gaze.

In contrast to his discretion about human beings, Old Tim laughed at the way dogs do sex—anytime, anywhere, no sense of kinship or taboo, and to top it off they get stuck. Their desire to stay in life, to stay connected, leads them into embarrassment and mortification. For that, he felt sorry for them. They know they are ridiculous and helpless, and there they are, right out in the middle of camp for all to see and laugh at. What with their howling at the threshold of life and death, their eating of corpses, and their public sex, dogs bring sex and death together in the most visible and stunningly extravagant ways. The dogs' outrageous excessiveness is *so dog*, and *so world*, *so* in the present, *so* in the face of human conventions, and thus forever a reminder of our connections within the world of life, lust, death, grief, and unbounded enthusiasms and desires.

Chapter 8, verse 6–7 is widely regarded as a key moment in the Song:

> *Bind me as a seal upon your heart,*
> *A sign upon your arm,*
>
> *For love is as fierce as death,*
> *Its jealousy bitter as the grave.*
> *Even its sparks are a raging fire,*
> *A devouring flame.*
>
> *Great seas cannot extinguish love,*
> *no river can sweep it away.*
>
> *If a man tried to buy love*
> *With all the wealth of his house,*
> *He would be despised.*

The equivalent strength of love and death is clearly stated. The assertion is situated within all this life, motion, connection, and fluidity. The Song of Songs is saying that it takes the whole erotic life of Earth, everything, all the flux and all the flow, to match the strength of death. There is an equivalence of love and death, and it depends on the whole living Earth singing up its erotic energy. The strength of love is the strength of Earth's erotic coming forth.

The Song tells us that death is fierce, but it does *not* tell us that death is the enemy. Quite the opposite, it seems to equate the relationship between love and death with the kind of fierce passion that exists between the lovers themselves. Sparks that cannot be extinguished by the seas equate love and death with elemental forces. In its fierce passion, the Song offers a wild sense of dynamic, far from equilibrium, balance.

How beautifully fluid is the whole Earth. Bloch and Bloch show us a poetics that patterns a fierce and tender relationship between death and love. The relationship is all about motion. The lovers take turns seeking one another: He invites her or "'goes down' to her; she goes looking for him or invites him. They move from desire to anticipation to fulfilment and back to desire; sexual consummation . . . is an episode in the poem, not its grand finale."[36] The Song gives us both return and departure, reveling in an erotic pattern that is of the Earth as well as of the lovers, and is perhaps not only the pattern of love, but equally the pattern of death and love as they interact with each other. Love and death embrace and depart, come together and withdraw, sustaining each other's passion.

Run away, my gazelle, my wild stag on the hills of cinnamon.

Nothing lasts forever: dogs know this too, and like us, they resist the knowledge. They want to live forever, and if they can't do that, they want to fuck forever. Even dogs get tired of that jealous hold, and that's the dilemma, for people and for dogs: we want to be together forever, and knowing we can't, we so desperately want to return. The return sings up eros, sings up the world, sings up life and holds it strong in the face of death.

Run away, my love, she calls, longing already to experience again, and yet again, the fierce and fiery return.

12. The Beginning Law

I have discussed many of the Western scientific and philosophical accounts of connectivity, and I have proposed an ecological erotics in which life and death are connected through departures and returns. Old Tim generally did things differently; his philosophical account of connectivity was a full-blown performance.

Cross-Species Returns

When I first arrived in Yarralin in 1980, I was given a house that for that time was up-to-date: a one-room corrugated iron shed with a tap in the yard and a covered veranda. Toilets and showers were shared by several families and were not far from my little house. I was near the center of the community, and the house was empty because a much-loved and -respected old man had died just a few days earlier. Only his dog remained, a sickly, sad-eyed creature who didn't last long. The funeral rituals were finished and the house had been smoked out, but no one wanted to move in. It was still too soon for people to have left the memories behind, and the grief of losing him was too strong. I was a stranger with no memories and no grief, and so the house became mine.

About a month later there was a funeral for another man who had died recently. It was a tense affair as there was a lot of bad feeling about the circumstances of his death. People were all on edge, and the mood of the place became more tense with every truck that arrived carrying angry people from other communities. I was immensely curious, but also aware that I knew almost nothing and understood even less. I sat on the veranda feeling torn between my desire to join in and my deep sense that I should keep out of it. Along came Old Tim. He sat with me and started talking, and he talked for hours. I took notes, as he was always keen for me to do. I listened to his stories, but part of my attention remained tuned to the sounds of wailing, fighting, and more wailing. My notes are something of a fugue: Old Tim's stories are interrupted with notes on what I was hearing of the funeral. I thought that Old Tim may have come to keep me away from the funeral by distracting me, and I was both grateful and annoyed.

Retrospectively, I am fascinated by his choice of stories. In counterpoint to the rituals of death and grief that surrounded us, Old Tim talked about coming into being. This was the moment when truly I began to "get it"—to understand the turning toward life that connects species and generations and brings death into dialogue. Already a few people had been telling me the history of how they came into their current life. One of the little girls who enjoyed talking to me, Aileen, had told me that she was a little lizard before she found her mother and father. Her friend Kathy also was a little lizard, and they used to play together in the bush until they found their way into their human families and became childhood friends.

Such stories constitute more-than-human genealogies that enmesh people in cross-species transformations. I came to learn that everyone had a history that told how their life came across through other species. Hobbles Danaiyarri, another of my great teachers, was a barramundi before he became a human. His father speared the fish, his mother ate some, and the spirit became the baby who grew into a gifted analyst and storyteller. On his right temple he had a small mark where his father speared the fish. In the early days, a group of Aboriginal people had been fishing and were shot up by Whitefellas. One of the men died in the water. His spirit became a barramundi; the barramundi became Hobbles. Happily, he had a large family to carry on after him, and he expected that his life would go through death, to become new life.

Old Tim's stories on that hot, tense afternoon offered a philosophy of connectivity not through abstractions but through engagement. Words and events became a contrapuntal performance. We will want to consider this pattern of engagement, but first let us listen to the stories. Sometimes Tim used the word "spirit" to talk about the will-to-life that moves from body to body. More often he used the word "kid," meaning the life that would become a human being. On the occasion of the long, angry funeral, he told me what would happen to the dead man. This involved introducing me to a hill nearby where dead people go and where kids hang out waiting for their opportunity to return: "Dead man, he gotta go to that hill and stop there at that hill. He'll come back. Those kids come from that hill. That's where the kids come from. All these kids come from that hill. When he's dead, he goes along to that place, stops five or seven years, then gets new mother, new daddy, gets born to them."

The Dingo ancestor was the originator of this Law (see chapter 7): "That kid find new father, new mother: that's the Dingo Law. . . . The dead man looks around, thinks about his Dreaming. . . . Makes himself into kangaroo, goanna, bird, crocodile. . . . That's the Law. From that Dog."

Tim went on to tell of the role of the clever man in this process, speaking himself into the story because the work that keeps the flow of life coming was an important part of his life: "Clever man—clever man can see that kid. 'Hey,' the clever man says to the kid, and the kid says, 'Which one is my mother, which one is my daddy?' The clever man shows him. The clever man is showing him that: 'You, that's your mother.' Showing the little kid that comes from the hill."

As the wailing continued, Old Tim talked about birth and about songs to make the baby be born quickly. Childbirth is the women's domain, but sometimes if the child is not coming, extra people are called on to help, even a man if he is clever. Mary Rutungali was a midwife, and both she and Old Tim had songs and techniques. Tim explained that when a woman was trying to give birth and was "just about dead," the attending women would ask for Mary. "I'm very tired, very tired, I can't do nothing," the birthing mother would say, and Mary would work on the woman's body and sing the songs. Similarly, if Tim was called, he'd sing and work with the power he had to help this life come. Within an hour or two, he said, the baby would be born, and would be crying with life. In the days before women were shipped away to hospital to give birth, people were born onto the ground. The blood of childbirth soaked into the earth (further details are not public knowledge in this region). Another of my teachers, Riley Young, explained the importance of birth and ground: "Aboriginal people bin born onto this ground . . . No hospital, no needle, no medicine . . . Because this ground is the hospital. Even me, I bin born onto this ground . . . I never bin born by top of the hospital. I bin born by ground."[1]

Another truck, more crying, and we paused to listen. Then Tim talked about songs to make the baby grow strong. He had done that for years too: sung songs from the Dreaming, giving the child the strength to walk. He spoke a bit about ceremonies for making boys into young men; about all the work that goes into making a human.

We sat on the veranda within earshot, but out of eyesight, of a funeral that went on and on. Old Tim was telling what would happen with this particular dead man, how this was the end of a life, but not the end of life altogether. Both philosophy and consolation were in his words. Looking back, I can see that Old Tim was offering a philosophy that brought birth and death together in creative dynamism. The philosophy was not strictly in the narrative; rather Old Tim worked with story and funeral to perform a philosophy. My notes show a pattern that took me years to come to understand, and that became most evident when we danced all night in the ceremony that makes a little boy into a young man.

Let us leave the funeral for a moment and think about dancing for life. The ceremony is called "Pantimi," and it was brought into the world by the Dreaming women who carried it out of the west. In these days, the men who are authorized to sing sit in a circle, and, using boomerangs as clapsticks, sing the songs. The women dance toward the men, moving from west to east and occasionally dancing around them. As we danced we were inscribing the ground with our feet. With each small song, we approached the circle of men. At each interval between the small songs, we withdrew, and when the song started up once more, we would again dance toward the singers. Our feet and legs produced a rhythm and our dance-call was a high-pitched vocal projection, also rhythmic. We worked the ground with our feet; we made tracks and raised dust, beating the rhythms of the dance right into the earth. Our call went out into the night to be heard not just by the Dreamings, but also by the dead and by all the living things who were not present but who would recognize the sounds of ceremony.

One of the outstanding patterns in Pantimi and other ceremonies is that of dance and non-dance. Between clusters of small songs there are large pauses. The rhythms of the song and dance are thus set within a larger oscillation of music and non-music. The non-music interval is dominated by joking. It is not a break in the ceremony but rather a contrapuntal engagement with the musical portion of the ceremony. One joke is topped by another, which is topped by another, and the jokes are spread out over the intervals so that the joking runs concurrently, carrying spontaneous inventive delight.

Ceremony thus works with two interwoven event types. The music and dance is Dreaming Law, and is complexly patterned; there are formal rules, and it must be performed correctly. The joking is a spontaneous commentary on daily life. Each joking interval is a qualitative and purposeful withdrawal from formality. Each song is a qualitative and purposeful return to Dreaming Law. The ethnomusicologist Cath Ellis describes Aboriginal music as "iridescent." She explains this unexpected concept with reference to the phenomenon that occurs when background and foreground suddenly flip. We all experience this in its visual form, particularly with art or photos that are designed to generate a visual/mental movement between background and foreground.[2] A familiar example is the visual illusion of faces or vases, where the image shifts from a vase or goblet to two people facing each other.[3]

This flip phenomenon is also experienced aurally, as one or another pattern is heard as foreground. Ellis states that the experience has several effects. It alters the perceived flow of time by interrupting recognized patterns, and it heightens one's awareness of the whole performance.[4] In the performance of ceremony, there are many flips. For the dancer there is the flip between the feet on the ground and the ground on the feet: Who is the dancer, and who is the danced? If we focus on motion, it is clear that both are dancer and danced, and that the significance of this mutuality is located in the flip back and forth between us.

The unpromisingly homely little term "flip" signals a deeply serious pattern that was present in ceremony and was present in Old Tim's philosophical performance of connectivity. If the funeral was the main theme, the story of birth was the counterpoint. If the stories of birth were the main theme, the cries of grief and anger were the counterpoint. But if both funeral and birth stories were main themes, what mattered was the flip back and forth between them. His masterly performance thus offered an account of death and birth, departure and return, and the mutuality of it all.

The pattern I want to focus on here is the play of the flip: two types of events, co-present, shaping and making each other, and participants flipping between them, foregrounding first one, then the other. Flips appear at first to be either/or: either this foreground or that foreground. But for participants, the patterns are experienced in the body and in time. One is experiencing both flow and simultaneity, and iridescence arises in the patterns of mutual copresence. Iridescence is the point at which the either/or is experienced as both/and. In thinking about life and death, we encounter just such an iridescence, a shimmer arising from Earth life. Time and multiplicity move us into flow. In terms of multiplicity, all living beings are in motion, coming or going, from place to place and from life to life. Equally, real life is situated in irreversible time. The flip is not an oscillation outside of time, but rather, as part of life, it works with the dynamics of disorder and creation. It is important to note that the philosophy of the flip runs counter to two important maxims that are current within contemporary spirituality movements. It is not possible that "we are all one" in flip philosophy. Differences must exist; there must be I and You, self and other, death and life, in order for there to be flips back and forth. Nor is it possible that "everything is connected to everything." It is the movement away that makes possible the movement toward. The unmaking and the making both matter. The flip is a pattern we have encountered around the campfire in the discussion of the death and transformation of Old Tim's father. The pattern depends on dynamics sustained within metamorphic flows of coming and going, turning and returning, birthing and dying.

The philosophy Old Tim performed had a name. He called it the Beginning Law. In what I came to appreciate as both inclusive generosity and confidence in his understanding of life, he said that all humans come into being through these processes of death and birth: "From beginning Dreaming, White man, Blackfella, Indian, any one, they're all born from that Beginning Law." His reasoning, as I understand it, was that this Law must be the same for everyone because this is how life is. Life wants to live, wants to be embodied, and keeps finding its way back into life. Life is always in a state of metamorphosis, across death into more life, crossing bodies, species, and generations. Through the juxtaposition of story and context, Old Tim affirmed metamorphosis in action, offering a philosophy of the will-to-life in which neither birth nor death is to be exclusively foregrounded. The movement back and forth is what enables life to shimmer and flourish. And while it is a Beginning Law in the sense of having been established in the Beginning, it is also a continuing law—this is how life is, it is always beginning. According to the Beginning Law, life and death are participatory and are kept in motion through cross-species transformations and returns. Old Tim's philosophy can surely be understood as a Law of Participation not unlike that which Lévy-Bruhl struggled to articulate (see chapter 10). The clever man didn't have to struggle to articulate his philosophy, however, because he was living and performing it. Against the background of Lévy-Bruhl's efforts, we can see that participatory "law" is, actually, participatory. Old Tim's masterful performance of flip captured the mutual embeddedness of birth and death, and it brought into awareness a deep connectivity that is the continuous becoming of the living world.

Creature Language

The Beginning Law comes from the Dingo, and like other Dingo stories it calls human beings into creatureliness and connection. The stories push humans toward participation, and in doing so they suggest that humans have a propensity for isolation. One of the most curious stories that Old Tim and others told concerns dingo behavior in relation to humans. When dingoes are by themselves in the bush, people said, they walk and talk like humans, but when humans come around they revert to dog shape and language. On the face of it, the story is similar to Dreaming stories in which all the creative beings originally walked in humanlike form. They were all shape-shifters, and they all spoke languages that are now human languages. But there did come a time of stabilization, and they all settled into the shapes and sounds of the familiar world. Clever people and animals can unsettle this stability, and Dreamings can be sung and danced into revitalized action, but only dingoes seem to have the ongoing capacity for shape-shifting. Their continuing capacity indicates that these creatures differ from the others. Moreover, their difference is contextualized. Only with humans do they refuse to come face-to-face in any form but canine. All the other creatures in the bush witness them in both forms; only humans are excluded.

These stories suggest an unexpected form of human exceptionalism. Western thought about the difference between humans and animals has characteristically turned on our exceptional (superior) status, a status marked by all that they (the others) don't do. Thus, we foresee death; they don't and therefore die insignificantly. We are self-aware; they are not and thus merely exist. We think; they run on instinct. We have logos; they don't. The list could go on for a long time. The point is that Old Tim's dingo stories offer a very different perspective, suggesting that humans are different because we, and only we, do not see dingo transformations. The one creature with whom we can reliably and predictably share names and language refuses to let us see how close we really are. How extraordinary!

The idea that we are exceptional on account of what we lack is taken up in an exquisite prose poem by the Australian poet Peter Boyle:

> Travelling in a caravan towards the World Capital where the Great King had invited him to speak at a symposium on the four elements, the philosopher let his mind drift from topic to topic, seeking an adequate response to present. Already they had crossed many lands and for some time now the unbounded sea ran alongside his meditations. The philosopher wanted to think of how we are in the world. The words "violence" and "loss" seemed essential to him, the words "cherishing" and "holding back." The sea the caravan journeyed beside stretched all the way to the island of dogs, the island where dogs cast aside by sailors had established their own community—a space little more than a sandbank where an immense loneliness ranged for here lived the dogs who had been cast out by humans.

> On the sandbank where the dogs lived the wild closeness of the stars generated the music of grief. Eventually the resonances of the music sealed the island off and, like many things that become too strong for human consciousness, it flickered inside and outside time, appearing and disappearing across the void, indifferent to the changing names of the millennia.

> He wondered in turn what would become of the people without
> dogs, those who sailed on to make new lands abandoning every-
> thing once cherished. Deciding that speech and closeness robbed
> them of marketable time, they developed a thing language to re-
> place the old creature languages. Instead of talking, they held up
> objects and compared one with another, and so stillness was ban-
> ished to the remotest distance.[5]

Boyle's prose poem dives into two huge effects of loss and shows how they are related. One effect is the impoverishment of humans who cast off Earth others and are left with nothing but objects. The other effect is the ongoing harmonics of connectivity (dogs and stars). The relationship works both ways in a negative synergy: as the dogs' harmonics of grief expand, the humans' capacity to discern them diminishes.

The pattern of cascading loneliness is familiar (see chapter 3), and we are left wondering how such a barrier might be breached. The story of how dingoes refuse to reveal themselves to humans may be understood in this context. The dingoes' insistence that if humans are to talk with other creatures they will have to understand and respond to creature languages can be understood as a move to curb the ever-present desire among humans to have it all their own way. Dogs could have formed a closed communicative world with humans from which all the others were excluded. In their shape and language-shifting, they are a constant reminder that if communication is to occur, people have to learn to understand the others. The "old creature language" that Boyle writes about forces us to take our attention away from a singular enchantment with our own kind of language, and to pay attention to the multitude of communicative registers—sounds, smells, behavior, the flowering trees, the seasons, the coming and going of birds, insects, and other creatures, the howling, and the silences too: all the myriad communication of living beings as they sing up themselves and their connectivities. Creature language is never monological; always relational, it is a call to enter into life-affirming dramas of encounter and recognition, to be inside the world, co-present, participatory, and engaged.

Dingo stories offer an account of humanity that is not particularly flattering, speaking as they do to our propensity for arrogance, triumph, and isolation. The story of the Moon is relevant not only in relation to death but also in relation to awareness of connectivity. The Moon knew he was alone, but in his arrogance he couldn't or wouldn't find a way out. Similarly, Job called God into dialogue, and although God spoke, he remained enthralled with his account of his own power. When we humans claim an exemption from connectivity, we slip into just such a place of arrogance, a place with no apparent way out.

The return into life through cross-species transformations suggests that the Beginning Law prevents us from thinking only about ourselves. Crossovers affirm the collaborative multispecies dynamics of birth and death. Indeed, the Beginning Law offers a deeper truth: that death is a move into connectivity. One way out of isolation is to accept the mortality of life on Earth. To accept mortality is to accept one's creaturely fate, and in the empathy of fate, to enter into call-and-response. Further, crossovers affirm the participatory quality of ethics. And even further, they affirm an Earth-based solidarity that embraces all of us—we whose bodies arise from the only ground we will ever know, ground that is saturated with the blood of birth as well as death.

Connectivity Ethics

Tim's work to bring new people into the world depended on songs and other knowledge that he had been given by old people who are now dead. Because the population loss during the period of initial invasion and for several decades afterward was so devastating (about 95 percent), he had become the repository of knowledge that had belonged to many people and countries, people who had no descendants and who desperately hoped to keep the knowledge alive in the world. Mary's songs had a similar genealogy. Only later did I learn that Tim and Mary had had no children of their own. Their work thus seemed to me to be acutely generous: they had experienced the extinction of many clans, and with no children to take over from them, their own future looked bleak. And still they worked to keep life coming.

So this is what it means to keep faith with life, I thought. Ethics within connectivity don't allow a person to give up. Life is always calling. When I think this, I have to remind myself that many people at Yarralin thought Old Tim was a bit crazy; he truly was a holy fool. In chapter 2, I suggested that if Old Tim's people had a first commandment, it might be: thou shalt not turn thine eyes away from the deaths of animals. To live in the world, to live in connectivity, is always to be living in proximity to death as well as to life, to cause death as well as to nurture life. The life that moves through us all does not give us morally unambiguous or pure sites to occupy. In a world of connectivity, there are no unambiguous rules such as "thou shalt not kill." We have already considered the main problems with this injunction. It cannot mean that humans must never kill; without death there could be no life. One response is to set up a boundary on one side of which killing is allowed, on the other side forbidden. The human-animal boundary is one way to make the cut about who can be killed with impunity. Another way is to put humans and animals together and exclude plants. One can refine the boundary by saying that killing can be acceptable provided there is no suffering, and so on. There is satisfaction in such rules—one can know how to keep one's hands clean. And of course I acknowledge that it is socially useful, indeed necessary, to have rules. But if we hold fast to relational principles, then we face a conceptualization of ethics based not on rules but on action. Relationally, purity is a delusional *as-if.* It is the refuge of those who do not want to face the fact that to live is to be part of it all: clear boundaries become an invitation to act *as if* there were a place of moral purity. Arguably, both the Moon and God (in relation to Job) could be thought to occupy such a place. It is not that they claim purity, but that in refusing connectivity they refuse responsibility and accountability, as the stories make amply clear. In contrast, the connectivities of life on Earth ensure that we are always called to face ambiguity and to act, to be responsible.

To be in relationship is to be vulnerable, as we have seen. The more we think about vulnerability, the clearer it becomes that the call of life within multispecies communities of fate must always contain both joy and grief, desire and loss. Shestov said something about this years ago, and I want to revisit his thoughts because they link multiplicity, shared suffering, existentialism, and craziness. The context of Shestov's great words is a rave against "reason," by which he means Certainty, scientific positivism, some forms of rationality, and other aspects of modernity that he dissected so vividly:

> If we turn to reason, we shall receive a finished philosophy of all-unity which satisfies our "theoretical need" and gives us truths obligatory for all and a morality obligatory for all. . . . If we do not recognise reason, then . . . from behind the comprehensible compelling truths which move obediently according to eternal laws within the boundaries of the unity of the universe, will break forth innumerable selfhoods that philosophy has kept in fetters during the course of thousands of years with their unsatisfied desires, with their inconsolable sorrows.[6]

In the face of these innumerable selfhoods with their calls of desire and grief, Shestov urges us "to learn anew to be horrified, to weep, to curse, to lose and find again the last hope". And that hope? That hope is the "enigmatic craziness" that he finds in relation to God,[7] and that I urge in relation to Earth. This kind of craziness, as I am learning, can also be understood and cherished as faithfulness in the face of all that is unknown and unknowable.

Connectivity ethics are open, uncertain, attentive, participatory, contingent. One is called upon to act, to engage in the dramas of call-and-response, and to do so on the basis of that which presents itself in the course of life. I am thinking of Old Tim chuckling to himself as he remembers the half-drowned White guy who wanted to know what happened. As I rehear the story again in my mind, I realize that Old Tim's action constitutes an ethical position. Levinas would have recognised this position, as would have Mencius.[8] Levinas would have seen the trace of God in the face of the drowning man; Mencius would have seen human empathy pressing Tim into action without the need for instrumental thought. Old Tim didn't engage in this kind of analysis, but he seems to have articulated a principle in his own clever way. He offers us the great "I don't know," a marvellous phrase that refuses justification and universalization. The ethical point of the story goes to Soulé's statement that people save what they love. We have seen that sometimes people do not save what they love, at least philosophically (see chapter 3). Now we see that some people also save that which they do not love. Old Tim saved the guy because the guy needed saving. There was no instrumental reason, no time to think through the reciprocities, no time to determine the rights and wrongs of things. Indeed, if Tim had thought the whole thing through, he might have come to the view that he didn't really want to save a man whose people had killed and dispossessed his, a man who in his own life and actions was an undesirable character from the point of view of the Aboriginal workers who were under his rule. If Tim had taken the time to think about it, he might have experienced thoughts such as these. I expect he would have saved the guy anyhow, but he seems to be telling us that he didn't think it through at all. He just did it. In refusing an overt decision-making process, he can be seen to be asserting a kind of love—a faithfulness to life in which call-and-response are yet another flip. Call-and-response, like life and death, are two types of events, co-present, shaping and making each other, and shaping and making the participants who flip back and forth, coming and going, calling and responding. The flip connects even as it differentiates. It is foundational to world making in a life-affirming awareness of uncertainty and connectivity.

Come Back

At this time, the rate of extinctions is somewhere between one thousand and ten thousand times the usual background rate as deduced from the fossil record. It is not possible to calculate with certainty the difference between the old usual rate and the current rate because we do not know how many species today are being eradicated. What we do know is that a rapidly expanding number of species is tipping into the "thin zone from the critically endangered to the living dead and thence into oblivion."[9]

People do want to save what they love, and perhaps one response to anthropogenic extinctions is to imagine that we can get by with loving less. As our world diminishes, so too might we harden our hearts to devastation, and proceed with yet another delusional *as if*—the delusion that we are not in connection and therefore that what happens doesn't concern us. We seem to do this well, but clearly it is a dead end. This much at least is certain: our lives are held in the hands of others; without them there is no us.

The call that crosses the zone of death—the great "come back" that we have howled for millennia—is the cry of love. Eros longs to remain in connection, but if love fails to be as fierce as death, death becomes ever more powerful. We are seeing deaths expand and expand, shifting into another state altogether. The current cascade of extinctions is drawing life out of Earth, unmaking the fabric of life, severing the bonds of connectivity. The numbers are terrible, and they aggregate an even more terrible fact: that extinctions are the result of many, many individual deaths, each one of which matters and many of which may have no future at all, ever.

That thin, scary zone where life and death brush close together is an opening wherein we are vividly called into ethics. The call is not on any grounds at all other than that there is peril, and there is power, and we are called. What happens? We don't have to know. We respond. We turn our faces toward the innumerable selfhoods of the living world, and we do what we can. Perhaps the most that can be said is that we encounter a wild and crazy ethic: we respond because we are here, because this opening occurred in our presence, because the zone is so thin, the lives so precious.

The Australian poet MTC Cronin seems to speak exactly toward these issues:

Whatever Becomes Itself
"Cada nivel tiene su propia irrigacion sanguinea"—Gloria Gervitz

"Every level has its own irrigation of blood," every level possesses a shudder, sway, sweet from the tips of the shadow, scug, cell passing, every emotion finds its own level, whatever becomes itself has that passion, *whatever becomes itself has that passion*, every thing finds its level, eyes, seeing life is seeing it going, eyes are sand, life, life is blood that moves, blood is sand, stars, stars are sand, every passion finds its level, cry warming itself in the blindness of blood, blood only flows in darkness, shudder, sway, sweetness of shadow, whatever becomes itself finds its own level, eyes, blood, stars and sand, and sand, sand becomes sand with the passion of eternity.[10]

The plummet toward some sort of level is a bloody cascade. And in the end the connective patterns between humans and others are open to emptiness too. The emptier Earth becomes, the emptier are those who remain alive. That emptiness may produce a particular gaze, a "mere life" gaze that refuses to live fully because it refuses to face all this death. The challenge, therefore, is to look into emptiness and, understanding the interdependence of life on earth, face the future. Will expanding death effects diminish us further as the life-sustaining capacities of Earth are degraded and extinguished? Is there a human tipping point? How much of our own humanity will we lose before we, too, collapse into irremediable loss?

Or perhaps we will reach out to make a difference. Perhaps voices from the death space *will speak* to us. If we could hear these harmonics, we would hear the call of those who are slipping out of life forever. There we might encounter a narrative emerging from extinctions, a level of blood that connects us rather than driving us apart. Such a narrative would enjoin us to rethink everything we thought we knew about who we are and how to live within the imperiled family of life on Earth.

Notes

1. Where Shall Wisdom Be Found?

1. www.colongwilderness.org.au/Dingo/Dingopage.htm.
2. Wilson, *The Future of Life*, 77.
3. Milton, "Fear for the Future."
4. Quoted in Ivan Doig, "West of the Hudson, Pronounced 'Wallace,'" 127.
5. See Rose, *Dingo Makes Us Human*.
6. See Rose, *Hidden Histories*.
7. Spoken by David Gulpilil in the biographical film (see Darlene Johnson, *Gulpilil: One Red Blood*).
8. Kepnes, *The Text as Thou*, 125.
9. Fackenheim, *To Mend the World*.
10. Shestov, *Athens and Jerusalem*, 63.
11. Ibid., 70.
12. Discussed in greater detail in Rose, *Hidden Histories*.
13. http://en.wikipedia.org/wiki/Rain_Dogs.
14. Jonas, *The Gnostic Religion*, 325.
15. Ibid., 290.
16. Ibid., 323–25.
17. Ibid., 327–30.
18. Kohak, *The Embers and the Stars*, 5.
19. Heidegger, "The Way Back into the Ground of Metaphysics," 214.
20. Buber, *Between Man and Man*, 167.
21. Quoted in Bauman, *Postmodern Ethics*, 221.
22. Kohak, "Varieties of Ecological Experience," 268.
23. Kohak, "The True and the Good," 291.
24. Newton, *Narrative Ethics*, 12.
25. Tsing, "Unruly Edges"; Shepard, *The Others*; Graham, "Some Thoughts on the Philosophical Underpinnings of Aboriginal Worldviews."
26. Eckersley, "Deliberative Democracy, Ecological Representation and Risk"; van Dooren, "Being-with-Death."
27. Hannah Arendt focused on the human sphere, but was not indifferent to the other-than-human world (see Arendt, *The Human Condition*). Donna Haraway uses the term "worlding" more than "world-making" (see Haraway, *When Species Meet*).
28. Newton, *Narrative Ethics*, 12.
29. Hatley, *Suffering Witness*, 24ff.
30. Abram, *The Spell of the Sensuous*.
31. Fackenheim, *To Mend the World*, 141.

32. Hearne, *Adam's Task*, 264.

33. "Transcript of Proceedings: North West Simpson Desert Land Claim (No. 126)," 317.

34. Oppenheim, *Speaking/Writing of God*, 54.

2. Looking into Extinction

1. Harvey, *Animism*, xi.

2. Rose, *Hidden Histories*, esp. chap. 9.

3. Prigogine, *The End of Certainty*, 158.

4. Margulis and Sagan, *What Is Life?* 55.

5. van Dooren, "Being-with-Death," 10.

6. Hatley, *Suffering Witness*.

7. Ibid., 212.

8. Ibid., 60–61.

9. See Rose, *Reports from a Wild Country*.

10. Agamben, *The Open*, among others.

11. This point is made by numerous authors: for hyperseparation, see Plumwood, *Feminism and the Mastery of Nature*; for animal-human naturecultures, see Haraway, *When Species Meet*.

12. Derrida, "The Animal That Therefore I Am (More to Follow)," 394.

13. Derrida is not the only scholar to make such juxtapositions, as I discuss in later chapters. I would note that Emmanuel Levinas touches briefly on the juxtaposition of the assembly-line death work in relation to animals and people, but turns away from an exploration of the deeper ethical questions by reinscribing an absolute boundary between people and nonhuman animals. David Clark, "On Being 'the Last Kantian in Nazi Germany,'" pursues this issue with great tact.

14. Derrida, "The Animal That Therefore I Am (More to Follow)," 394.

15. Derrida, discussed in Clark, "On Being 'the Last Kantian in Nazi Germany,'" 176.

16. Ibid., 171.

17. Ibid.

18. Quoted in Gray, *Abrogating Responsibility*.

19. Ibid.

20. Discussed in detail in Wyschogrod, *Emmanuel Levinas*, 229.

21. Clark, "On Being 'the Last Kantian in Nazi Germany,'" 185.

22. Derrida, "The Animal That Therefore I Am (More to Follow)," 394.

23. Bauman, *Wasted Lives*, 39.

3. Bobby's Face, My Love

1. Levinas, "Name of a Dog, or Natural Rights," 152.

2. Ibid., 153.

3. Clark, "Towards a Prehistory of the Postanimal."

4. For example: Casper, "Responsibility Rescued"; Grob, "Emmanuel Levinas

and the Primacy of Ethics in Post-Holocaust Philosophy"; and Rose, *Reports from a Wild Country.*

5. Excellent essays on Bobby include: Atterton, "Face-to-Face with the Other Animal?"; Cavalieri, "A Missed Opportunity"; and Wolfe, *Animal Rites.*

6. Llewelyn, "Am I Obsessed by Bobby?" 237.

7. Clark, "On Being 'the Last Kantian in Nazi Germany,'" 190–91.

8. Steeves, "Lost Dog," 53.

9. Agamben, for example, argues in *The Open* that our metaphysics have been predicated on sustaining the meaning of humanity through an oppositional contrast between humans and animals.

10. Quoted in Fackenheim, *To Mend the World,* 273.

11. Bauman, "The Holocaust's Life as a Ghost," 13, 14.

12. In a recent unpublished essay, David Clark, "Towards a Prehistory of the Post-animal," offers a slow and generous reading of this essay that enables a beautifully nuanced engagement with Levinas.

13. *Tanakh: The Holy Scriptures.* There are some variations in the translation of what the dogs are required not to do: my version uses the term "snarl"; Levinas uses the term "growl," and other scholars, for example Steeves, engage in deeper analysis of the Hebrew words. The consensus is, however, that the dogs are silenced.

14. Levinas, "Name of a Dog, or Natural Rights," 152.

15. Schwartz, *The Curse of Cain.*

16. Alter, *The Art of Biblical Narrative.*

17. Soloveitchik, *The Lonely Man of Faith,* 9–26.

18. Amichai, "On the Night of the Exodus."

19. Coetzee, *Disgrace,* 146. Hereafter cited parenthetically in the text.

20. See also Hacking, "Our Fellow Animals," 24.

21. Quoted in Oppenheim, *Speaking/Writing of God,* 54.

22. Irigaray, "Questions to Emmanuel Levinas," 182.

23. Oppenheim, *Speaking/Writing of God,* 54.

24. It may be asking too much of people incarcerated in concentration camps that they embrace the sensuous world, although rare folk like Viktor Frankl, *Man's Search for Ultimate Meaning,* have managed it. I should reiterate that Levinas wrote this essay thirty years after the event.

25. Derrida, "The Animal That Therefore I Am (More to Follow)," 399.

4. Ecological Existentialism

1. Martin, "Introduction."

2. Shestov, *Athens and Jerusalem,* 180.

3. Herberg, *Four Existentialist Theologians,* 2.

4. Jonas, *The Gnostic Religion,* 323.

5. Soloveitchik, *The Lonely Man of Faith,* 70. The gendered quality of much of this theology is discussed by several superb feminist thinkers (see, for example, Plaskow, *Standing Again at Sinai*).

6. Haraway, *When Species Meet;* Tsing, "Unruly Edges."
7. Shestov, "Myth and Truth," 73.
8. Plato, *Phaedrus,* 78.
9. Shestov, *Athens and Jerusalem,* 65.
10. Ibid., 65.
11. Shestov, *Speculation and Revelation,* 47.
12. Quoted in Dietrich, *The Final Forest,* 110.
13. Summarized in Mellor, *Feminism and Ecology.*
14. Ciancio and Nocentini, "Forest Management from Positivism to the Culture of Complexity."
15. Prigogine, *The End of Certainty,* 19–27.
16. Discussed in detail in Plumwood, *Feminism and the Mastery of Nature.*
17. Margulis and Sagan, *What Is Life?* 226.
18. Hoffmeyer, *Signs of Meaning in the Universe,* 24.
19. Bateson, *Steps to an Ecology of Mind,* 436–37.
20. Prigogine, *The End of Certainty,* 72.
21. Margulis and Sagan, *What Is Life?* 86.
22. Ibid., 191.

5. Orion's Dog

1. Robinson, *Altjeringa and Other Aboriginal Poems,* 25.
2. Twain, "Following the Equator."
3. Leithauser, "Zodiac: A Farewell."
4. Hearne, *Animal Happiness,* 97.
5. Dianne Johnson, "The Pleiades in Australian Aboriginal and Torres Strait Islander Astronomies," 24–28; see page 26 for this story.
6. Twain, *The Adventures of Tom Sawyer and the Adventures of Huckleberry Finn,* 49.
7. Quoted in Hasel, "The Origin and Early History of the Remnant Motif in Ancient Israel," 90.
8. On wolf howling, see Lopez, *Of Wolves and Men,* 38–39.
9. www.dingoconservation.org.
10. Quoted from a postcard advertising Stuart's Well Roadhouse and Caravan Park.
11. Dowe and McNaughton, "Rivers of Babylon," 63.

6. Singing Up the Others

1. Shepard, *The Others,* 11.
2. Ibid., 118–19.
3. Haraway, *When Species Meet,* 3.
4. Shepard, *The Others,* 119.
5. Leopold, *A Sand County Almanac,* 224–25.
6. Margulis and Sagan, *What Is Life?* 43.
7. Ibid., 17, 31.

8. Ibid., 17.

9. Ibid., 31; Haraway, *When Species Meet,* 32–33.

10. Margulis and Sagan, *What Is Life?* 31.

11. Ibid., 156–57.

12. Ibid., 91.

13. Ibid., 144.

14. Ibid., 91.

15. Quamman, *The Song of the Dodo,* 528.

16. Mathews, "Ceres: Singing up the City."

17. At the time that dingoes arrived on mainland Australia, the island of Tasmania was completely isolated. Dogs arrived in Tasmania in numbers only with European settlement. It has been possible through written records to gain an understanding of the first encounters between Aboriginal people and dogs, an encounter that was full of enthusiasm on the part of the people, and most probably on the part of the dogs as well (see Jones, "Tasmanian Aborigines and Dogs").

18. O'Neill, *Living with the Dingo,* 13.

19. Lopez, *Of Wolves and Men.*

20. Alternatives such as building better fences around sheep paddocks bump up against the pastoralist ideology that they should be able to do anything to protect the interests of their domesticated animals, and that anything that impinges on their usual practices is an infringement of their natural rights. As one encounters these people in newspaper accounts, Web sites and casual conversations, they speak from what seems to be a totalizing worldview of extreme positions: anything that threatens their livestock has to go.

21. In Rose, *Dingo Makes Us Human,* 91.

22. Woodford, *The Dog Fence,* 1.

23. Ibid., 6.

24. Ibid., 68.

25. Ibid., 70 (both quotes).

26. There has been speculation that native species have a high tolerance for the substance. It turns out that the high tolerance among native animals is concentrated in the state of Western Australia, where plants contain higher levels of the substance. Throughout most of Australia, 1080 is harmful to native species, and in some areas, as with plantation forestry, is specifically used to combat them.

27. ABC, "Farming Poison Puts Tasmania's Native Animals at Risk."

28. Pickard, "Predator-Proof Fences for Biodiversity Conservation," 202.

29. Discussed in Wallach and O'Neill, "Persistence of Endangered Species," 14.

30. Discussion summarized from Johnson, *Australia's Mammal Extinctions.*

31. O'Neill, *Living with the Dingo,* 105.

32. Wallach and O'Neill, "Persistence of Endangered Species," 43–44.

33. O'Neill, *Living with the Dingo,* 33.

34. Wallach and O'Neill, "Persistence of Endangered Species," 31.

35. O'Neill, *Living with the Dingo*, 36.
36. A further result may be an increase in numbers of dogs who are a dingo/feral domesticate mix. O'Neill contends that when families are stable, there is little opportunity for feral dogs to mate with dingoes because the alpha male and female will not allow intruders. But if the family is broken up, there are lone creatures looking for partners, and ferals have a greater opportunity to breed (ibid., 38).
37. David Jenkins, quoted in Beeby, "Genetic Dilution Dogs Dingoes," 5.
38. Lopez, *Of Wolves and Men*, 199.

7. Job's Grief

1. The book of Job is a "classic": it keeps pulling us back, and it continues to speak to us (Schreiner, *Where Shall Wisdom Be Found?*). I cannot attempt to engage with the past literature on Job. My purpose, more modestly, is to bring Job into the region of an Aboriginal story and to reimagine Job through that story.
2. Habel, "Earth First," 67.
3. Job 30:20, *Tanakh*. I use italics to indicate direct speech.
4. Shestov, *Speculation and Revelation*, 246–50.
5. Job 19:3, 19, *Tanakh*.
6. Sebald, "Campo Santo," 7.
7. Ibid., 7.
8. Job 7:9–10, Mitchell, *Into the Whirlwind*, 29.
9. Habel, "Earth First," 70.
10. Hallote, *Death, Burial and Afterlife in the Biblical World*, 6.
11. The difference between house and lineage is interestingly analyzed by Mieke Bal, *Death and Dissymmetry*.
12. Job 17:15–16, *Tanakh*.
13. Habel, "Earth First," 73.
14. Taylor, "The Origins of the Mastiff."
15. Job 38:4–7, Mitchell, *Into the Whirlwind*, 83.
16. Job 42:2. Habel, in his study *The Book of Job*, 577–80, offers a concise summary of the main ways of interpreting the tenor of Job's words, including the possibility of sarcasm.

8. What If the Angel of History Were a Dog?

1. Benjamin, *Illuminations*, 257–58.
2. Wyschogrod, *Spirit in Ashes*.
3. Parfit, "The Puzzle of Reality," 420.
4. Dostoevsky, *The Grand Inquisitor*, 13.
5. Ibid., 14.
6. Guignon, introduction to *The Grand Inquisitor*, by Dostoyevsky, xxix.
7. Ibid., xxx.
8. Shestov, *Speculation and Revelation*, 245–47.

9. Wiesel, "Job: Our Contemporary," 233–34.

10. Ibid., 233.

11. Ibid., 235.

12. "1080 Poison"; "Safe Use of 1080 Poison."

13. Hatley, *Suffering Witness,* 60–61.

14. Ibid., 61.

15. Ibid., 23.

16. Ibid., 70.

17. Ibid., 63.

18. Ibid.

19. Margulis and Sagan, *What Is Life?* 31.

20. Ibid., 98.

21. Ibid., 5.

22. Ibid., 238.

23. Ibid., 191.

24. Ibid., 22.

25. Benjamin, *Illuminations,* 258.

26. Edgar, "Chernobyl Dogs," 35–39.

27. On community of fate, see Eckersley, "Deliberative Democracy, Ecological Representation and Risk."

28. See Rose, *Reports from a Wild Country,* chap. 9.

29. Although 1080 is often claimed to cause a "humane" death, recent evidence indicates that terrible suffering may be experienced (see Wallach and O'Neill, "Persistence of Endangered Species").

30. Hacking, "Our Fellow Animals," 24.

31. Levinas, when pressed, argued against causing suffering to animals (in Atterton, "Face-to-Face with the Other Animal?" 271).

9. Ruined Faces

1. Lopez, *Of Wolves and Men.*

2. Scarry, *The Body in Pain,* 7; Hatley, *Suffering Witness,* 77–78.

3. Wiesel, "A Plea for the Dead," 229.

4. Hatley, *Suffering Witness,* 63.

5. Personal communication. The names of the dingoes: Murlanijarri and Yirilijpungu.

6. Martin, *Great Twentieth Century Jewish Philosophers,* 26.

7. Guiding scholars here are Zachary Braiterman, *(God) after Auschwitz,* and Richard L. Rubenstein, *After Auschwitz,* but the ripples caused by this question go well beyond theology.

8. Levinas, "The Paradox of Morality," 175–76; see the elegant discussion by Tamra Wright, "Beyond the 'Eclipse of God.'"

9. Levinas, "Name of a Dog, or Natural Rights," 153.

10. Fagenblat, "Back to the Other Levinas"; Fagenblat, "Creation and Covenant in Levinas' Philosophical Midrash."

11. Levinas, "Martin Buber and the Theory of Knowledge," 20. Levinas's purpose in this essay is to work with Buber's theory of knowledge, and thus the question I pursue here is peripheral to his purposes.

12. Levinas, "Name of a Dog, or Natural Rights," 153.

13. Linke, *Blood and Nation*, vii–xiii, 211.

14. Fagenblat, "Back to the Other Levinas," 299.

15. Discussed in detail in Kaplan, "The Metapolitics of Power and Conflict," 71.

16. Hatley, *Suffering Witness*, 62–64.

17. Fackenheim, *To Mend the World*, 75.

18. Rigby, *Topographies of the Sacred*, 48–54.

19. "Aenocide" is Hatley's insightful term (Hatley, *Suffering Witness*, 30–31).

20. Tumarkin, *Traumascapes*, 190.

21. Boyle, *Apocrypha*, 231–32.

10. World-Crazy

1. Rose, *Dingo Makes Us Human*.

2. Barnard, *History and Theory in Anthropology*, 106–7.

3. Shestov, "Myth and Truth," 124, 125.

4. Lévy-Bruhl, *Primitive Mythology*, 29.

5. Lévy-Bruhl, *How Natives Think*, 77–78.

6. Ibid., 69–104.

7. Abram, *The Spell of the Sensuous*, 57. Abram links participation with perception in the work of Merleau-Ponty, offering an analysis with which I plan to engage more fully in another publication.

8. Shestov, "Myth and Truth," 126.

9. Prigogine, *The End of Certainty*, 62.

10. Ibid., 72.

11. Quoted ibid., 11.

12. Plumwood, *Feminism and the Mastery of Nature*, 96.

13. Ibid., 89–102.

14. Quoted in Rose, *Dingo Makes Us Human*, 70–71. In this version I have changed Tim's Aboriginal Pastoral English into a more standard English, while striving to retain the flavor of his words.

15. Haraway, *When Species Meet*, 367–68.

16. Ibid., 368.

17. Shestov, *Speculation and Revelation*, 70.

18. Mathews, *For Love of Matter*, 161–77.

19. Haraway, *When Species Meet*, 71.

20. Mathews, *For Love of Matter*, 48, 61.

21. Shestov, "Speculation and Apocalypse," 87–88, and elsewhere.

11. Solomon's Wisdom

1. Thubron, *The Lost Heart of Asia*, 262.

2. Plumwood, "Tasteless"; Plumwood, "Being Prey."

3. Crossan, "The Dogs beneath the Cross."

4. Fadhil, "City of Ghosts."

5. Bloch and Bloch, *The Song of Songs*, 10.

6. Crenshaw, *Old Testament Wisdom*, 3.

7. Bloch and Bloch, *The Song of Songs*, 3.

8. Alter, "The Garden of Metaphor," 139.

9. Bloch and Bloch, *The Song of Songs*, 9–10.

10. Holler, *Erotic Orality*, 3.

11. Alter, afterword to *The Song of Songs*.

12. Mathews, *For Love of Matter*, 60.

13. Song of Songs 2:2; Bloch and Bloch, *The Song of Songs*, 55; this and other quotes are taken from Bloch and Bloch, *The Song of Songs*.

14. Alter, "The Garden of Metaphor."

15. Bloch and Bloch, *The Song of Songs*, 4:16.

16. Ibid., 1:12; 6:11; 1:16.

17. Ibid., 8:6–7.

18. Phipps, "The Plight of the Song of Songs," 23.

19. See Whaley, introduction to *Mirrors of Mortality*, ed. Whaley.

20. Quoted in Davies, *Death, Burial and Rebirth in the Religions of Antiquity*, 119.

21. Quoted ibid., 78–79.

22. Pope, "Interpretations of the Sublime Song," 45.

23. Ibid., 33.

24. Ibid., 33.

25. Ibid., 47.

26. The "dog under the couch" is a widespread motif; one longs for more research. For an excellent recent analysis, see Cadwallader, "When a Woman Is a Dog."

27. Morey, "Burying Key Evidence," 165–66.

28. Ibid., 161, 164.

29. Eriksen, "Motivations for Pet-Keeping in Ancient Greece and Rome," 29, 33.

30. Boyce, "Dog in Zoroastrianism."

31. Dunn, "The Dogs of Ancient Egypt."

32. Hansen, "Indo-European Views of Death and the Afterlife," 176.

33. Boyce, "Dog in Zoroastrianism."

34. Boyce, *A History of Zoroastrianism*, 120.

35. In Pope, "Interpretations of the Sublime Song," 28.

36. Bloch and Bloch, *The Song of Songs*, 17.

12. The Beginning Law

1. Full quote in Rose, *Dingo Makes Us Human*, 62.

2. Ellis, "Time Consciousness of Aboriginal Performers," 168.

3. See http://www.uic.edu/com/eye/LearningAboutVision/EyeSite/OpticalIllus tions/FaceVase.shtml for one example of this illusion.

4. Ellis, "Time Consciousness of Aboriginal Performers," 160, 168–69.

5. Boyle, "Travelling in a Caravan."

6. Shestov, *Speculation and Revelation*, 85.

7. Ibid., 87.

8. Rose, "'Moral Friends' in the Zone of Disaster."

9. Wilson, *The Future of Life*, 90.

10. Cronin, "Whatever Becomes Itself."

Bibliography

ABC. "Farming Poison Puts Tasmania's Native Animals at Risk." Australia, 2001. ABC Television transcript, Broadcast 17 April 2001. www.abc.net.au/7.30/content/2001/s278482.htm.

Abram, David. *The Spell of the Sensuous: Perception and Language in a More-Than-Human World*. New York: Vintage Books, 1996.

Agamben, Giorgio. *The Open: Man and Animal*. Translated by Kevin Attell. Stanford, Calif.: Stanford University Press, 2004.

Alter, Robert. Afterword to *The Song of Songs. With an Introduction and Commentary*, 119–36. Berkeley and Los Angeles: University of California Press, 1995.

———. *The Art of Biblical Narrative*. London: Allen and Unwin, 1981.

———. "The Garden of Metaphor." In *The Song of Songs*, edited by Harold Bloom, 121–39. New York: Chelsea House, 1988.

Amichai, Yehuda. "On the Night of the Exodus." Translated by Chana Bloch and Chana Kronfeld. *New York Review of Books* 46, no. 6 (1999): 9.

Arendt, Hannah. *The Human Condition*. Chicago: University of Chicago Press, 1958.

Atterton, Peter. "Face-to-Face with the Other Animal?" In *Levinas & Buber: Dialogue & Difference*, edited by Atterton, Matthew Calarco, and Maurice Friedman, 262–81. Pittsburgh: Duquesne University Press, 2004.

Bal, Mieke. *Death and Dissymmetry: The Politics of Coherence in the Book of Judges*. Chicago: University of Chicago Press, 1988.

Barnard, Alan. *History and Theory in Anthropology*. Cambridge: Cambridge University Press, 2000.

Bateson, Gregory. *Steps to an Ecology of Mind*. London: Granada, 1973.

Bauman, Zygmunt. "The Holocaust's Life as a Ghost." In *The Holocaust's Life as a Ghost: Writing on Arts, Politics, Law and Education*, edited by F. C. Dacoste and Bernard Schwartz, 3–15. Edmonton: University of Alberta Press, 2000.

———. *Postmodern Ethics*. Oxford: Blackwell, 1993.

———. *Wasted Lives: Modernity and Its Outcasts*. Oxford: Polity Press, 2004.

Beeby, Rossyln. "Genetic Dilution Dogs Dingoes." *Canberra Times*, 2 July 2007.

Benjamin, Walter. *Illuminations*. Translated by Harry Zohn; edited by Hannah Arendt. New York: Schocken Books, 1969.

Bloch, Ariel, and Chana Bloch. *The Song of Songs: A New Translation with an Introduction and Commentary*. Berkeley and Los Angeles: University of California Press, 1995.

Boyce, Mary. "Dog in Zoroastrianism." *The Circle of Ancient Iranian Studies*. 1998. www.cais-soas.com/CAIS/Animals/dog_zoroastrian.htm.

———. *A History of Zoroastrianism.* Leiden: Brill, 1975.

Boyle, Peter. *Apocrypha: Texts Collected and Translated by William O'Shaunessy.* Sydney: Vagabond Press, 2009.

———. "Travelling in a Caravan." *Australian Humanities Review,* no. 39–40 (2006). www.australianhumanitiesreview.org/archive/Issue-September-2006/boyle. html.

Braiterman, Zachary. *(God) after Auschwitz: Tradition and Change in Post-Holocaust Jewish Thought.* Princeton, N.J.: Princeton University Press, 1998.

Buber, Martin. *Between Man and Man.* Translated by Ronald Smith. London: Kegan Paul, 1947.

Cadwallader, Allan. "When a Woman Is a Dog: Ancient and Modern Ethology Meet the Syrophoenician Women." *Bible and Critical Theory* 1, no. 4 (2005): 35.1–35.17.

Casper, Bernhard. "Responsibility Rescued." In *The Philosophy of Franz Rosenzweig,* edited by Paul Mendes-Flohr, 89–106. Hanover, N.H.: University Press of New England, 1988.

Cavalieri, Paola. "'A Missed Opportunity': Humanism, Anti-Humanism and the Animal Question." In *Animal Subjects: An Ethical Reader in a Posthuman World,* edited by Jodey Castriciano, 97–123. Ontario: Wilfrid Laurier University Press, 2008.

Ciancio, O., and S. Nocentini. "Forest Management from Positivism to the Culture of Complexity." In *Methods and Approaches in Forest History,* edited by M. Agnoletti and S. Anderson, 47–58. Wallingford, U.K.: CABI, 2000.

Clark, David. "On Being 'the Last Kantian in Nazi Germany': Dwelling with Animals after Levinas." In *Animal Acts: Configuring the Human in Western History,* edited by Jennifer Ham and Matthew Senior, 165–98. New York: Routledge, 1999.

———. "Towards a Prehistory of the Postanimal: Kant, Levinas, and the Regard of Brutes." Manuscript. 2006.

Coetzee, J. M. *Disgrace.* London: Vintage Books, 2000.

Crenshaw, James. *Old Testament Wisdom: An Introduction.* Louisville: Westminster John Knox Press, 1998.

Cronin, M. T. C. "Whatever Becomes Itself." *Australian Humanities Review,* no. 39–40 (2006). www.australianhumanitiesreview.org/archive/Issue-September-2006/cronin.html.

Crossan, John Dominic. "The Dogs beneath the Cross." In *Jesus: A Revolutionary Biography.* New York: HarperCollins, 1994.

Davies, Jon. *Death, Burial and Rebirth in the Religions of Antiquity.* London: Routledge, 1999.

Derrida, Jacques. "The Animal That Therefore I Am (More to Follow)." *Critical Inquiry* 28, no. 2 (2002): 369–418.

Dietrich, William. *The Final Forest: The Battle for the Last Great Trees of the Pacific Northwest.* New York: Penguin Books, 1992.

Doig, Ivan. "West of the Hudson, Pronounced 'Wallace.'" In *The Geography of*

Hope: A Tribute to Wallace Stegner, edited by Page Stegner and Mary Stegner, 125–29. San Francisco: Sierra Club Books, 1996.

Dostoevsky, Fyodor. *The Grand Inquisitor: With Related Chapters from the Brothers Karamazov.* Indianapolis: Hackett, 1993.

Dowe, Brent, and Trevor McNaughton. "Rivers of Babylon." In *Rise up Singing,* edited by Peter Blood and Annie Patterson, 63. Bethlehem, Pa.: Sing Out Publications, 1992.

Dunn, Jimmy. "The Dogs of Ancient Egypt." www.touregypt.net/featurestories/dogs.htm.

Eckersley, Robyn. "Deliberative Democracy, Ecological Representation and Risk: Toward a Democracy of the Affected." In *Democratic Innovation: Deliberation, Representation and Association,* edited by Michael Saward, 117–32. London: Routledge, 2000.

Edgar, Stephen. "Chernobyl Dogs." In *Where the Trees Were.* Canberra: Ginninderra Press, 1999.

Ellis, Cath. "Time Consciousness of Aboriginal Performers." In *Problems and Solutions: Occasional Essays in Musicology Presented to Alice M. Moyle,* edited by Jamie Kassler and Jill Stubington, 149–85. Sydney: Hale and Iremonger, 1984.

Eriksen, Philippe. "Motivations for Pet-Keeping in Ancient Greece and Rome: A Preliminary Survey." In *Companion Animals and Us: Exploring the Relationship between People and Pets,* edited by Anthony Podberscek and Elizabeth Paul, 27–41. New York: Cambridge University Press, 2000.

Fackenheim, Emil. *To Mend the World: Foundations of Post-Holocaust Jewish Thought.* Bloomington: Indiana University Press, 1994.

Fadhil, Ali. "City of Ghosts." *Guardian,* 11 January 2005. www.guardian.co.uk/world/2005/jan/11/iraq.features11.

Fagenblat, Michael. "Back to the Other Levinas: Reflections Prompted by Alain P. Toumayan's *Encountering the Other: The Artwork and the Problem of Difference in Blanchot and Levinas.*" *Colloquy* 10 (2005): 298–313.

———. "Creation and Covenant in Levinas' Philosophical Midrash." Paper presented at the Bible and Critical Theory Seminar, Melbourne, Australia, 2006.

Frankl, Viktor. *Man's Search for Ultimate Meaning.* New York: Perseus, 2000.

Graham, Mary. "Some Thoughts on the Philosophical Underpinnings of Aboriginal Worldviews." *Australian Humanities Review,* no. 45 (2008).

Gray, Geoffrey. *Abrogating Responsibility: Vesteys, Anthropology and the Future of Aboriginal People.* Melbourne: Australian Publishing Company, 2010.

Grob, Leonard. "Emmanuel Levinas and the Primacy of Ethics in Post-Holocaust Philosophy." In *Ethics after the Holocaust: Perspectives, Critiques, and Responses,* edited by John Roth, 1–14. St Paul, Minn.: Paragon House, 1999.

Guignon, Charles. Introduction to *The Grand Inquisitor,* by Fyodor Dostoevsky. Indianapolis: Hackett, 1993.

Habel, Norman. *The Book of Job: A Commentary.* Philadelphia: Westminster Press, 1985.

———. "Earth First: Inverse Cosmology in Job." In *The Earth Story in Wisdom Traditions*, edited by Norman Habel and Shirley Wurst, 65–77. Sheffield: Sheffield Academic Press, 2001.

Hacking, Ian. "Our Fellow Animals." *New York Review of Books* 29, no. 11 (2000): 20–26.

Hallote, Rachel. *Death, Burial and Afterlife in the Biblical World.* Chicago: Ivan R. Dee, 2001.

Hansen, Leigh Jellison. "Indo-European Views of Death and the Afterlife as Determined from Archaeological, Mythological and Linguistic Sources." Ph.D. diss., University of California, 1987.

Haraway, Donna. *When Species Meet.* Minneapolis: University of Minnesota Press, 2008.

Harvey, Graham. *Animism: Respecting the Living World.* New York: Columbia University Press, 2006.

Hasel, Gerhard. "The Origin and Early History of the Remnant Motif in Ancient Israel." Ph.D. diss., Vanderbilt University, 1970.

Hatley, James. *Suffering Witness: The Quandary of Responsibility after the Irreparable.* Albany: State University of New York Press, 2000.

Hearne, Vicki. *Adam's Task: Calling Animals by Name.* Pleasantville, N.Y.: Akadine Press, 2000.

———. *Animal Happiness: A Moving Exploration of Animals and Their Emotions.* New York: Harper Perennial, 1995.

Heidegger, Martin. "The Way Back into the Ground of Metaphysics." In *Existentialism from Dostoevsky to Sartre*, edited by Walter Kaufman, 206–21. New York: Meridian Books, 1949.

Herberg, Will. *Four Existentialist Theologians: A Reader from the Works of Jacques Maritain, Nicolas Berdyaev, Martin Buber, and Paul Tillich.* Garden City: Doubleday, 1958.

Hoffmeyer, Jesper. *Signs of Meaning in the Universe.* Translated by Barbara Haveland. Bloomington: Indiana University Press, 1993.

Holler, Linda. *Erotic Orality: The Role of Touch in Moral Agency.* New Brunswick, N.J.: Rutgers University Press, 2002.

Irigaray, Luce. "Questions to Emmanuel Levinas: On the Divinity of Love." In *Re-Reading Levinas*, edited by Robert Bernasconi and Simon Critchley, 109–18. London: Athlone, 1991.

Johnson, Chris. *Australia's Mammal Extinctions: A 50,000-Year History.* New York, Cambridge, and Port Melbourne: Cambridge University Press, 2006.

Johnson, Darlene, dir. *Gulpilil: One Red Blood.* Australia: Ronin Films, 2007.

Johnson, Dianne. "The Pleiades in Australian Aboriginal and Torres Strait Islander Astronomies." In *The Oxford Companion to Aboriginal Art and Culture*, edited by S. Kleinert and M. Neale, 24–28. Melbourne: Oxford University Press, 2000.

Jonas, Hans. *The Gnostic Religion.* Boston: Beacon Press, 2001.

Jones, Rhys. "Tasmanian Aborigines and Dogs." *Mankind* 7 (1970): 256–71.

Kaplan, H. "The Metapolitics of Power and Conflict." In *The Holocaust's Ghost: Writing on Art, Politics, Law and Education,* edited by F. C. Decoste and Bernard Schwartz, 65–74. Edmonton: University of Alberta Press, 2000.

Kepnes, Steven. *The Text as Thou: Martin Buber's Dialogical Hermeneutics and Narrative Theology.* Bloomington: Indiana University Press, 1992.

Kohak, Erazim. *The Embers and the Stars: A Philosophical Inquiry into the Moral Sense of Nature.* Chicago: University of Chicago Press, 1984.

———. "The True and the Good: Reflections on the Primacy of Practical Reason." In *Philosophies of Nature: The Human Dimension,* edited by R. S. Cohen and A. I. Tauber, 209–19. London: Kluwer Academic Publishers, 1988.

———. "Varieties of Ecological Experience." In *Philosophies of Nature: The Human Dimension,* edited by R. S. Cohen and A. I. Tauber, 257–71. London: Kluwer Academic Publishers, 1998.

Leithauser, Brad. "Zodiac: A Farewell." *New York Review of Books* 51, no. 18 (2004): 16–17.

Leopold, Aldo. *A Sand County Almanac.* London: Oxford University Press, 1949.

Levinas, Emmanuel. "Martin Buber and the Theory of Knowledge." In *Proper Names,* by Levinas, 17–35. London: Athlone Press, 1996.

———. "Name of a Dog, or Natural Rights." In *Difficult Freedom: Essays on Judaism,* 151–53. Baltimore: Johns Hopkins University Press, 1990.

———. "The Paradox of Morality: An Interview with Emmanuel Levinas." In *The Provocation of Levinas: Rethinking the Other,* edited by Robert Bernasconi and David Woods, 168–80. London and New York: Routledge, 1988.

Lévy-Bruhl, Lucien. *How Natives Think.* Translated by Lilian Clare. London: George Allen and Unwin, 1926.

———. *Primitive Mythology: The Mythic World of the Australian and Papuan Natives.* Translated by Brian Elliott. St Lucia: Queensland University Press, 1983.

Linke, Uli. *Blood and Nation: European Aesthetics of Race.* Philadelphia: University of Pennsylvania Press, 1999.

Llewelyn, John. "Am I Obsessed by Bobby? (Humanism of the Other Animal)." In *Re-Reading Levinas,* edited by Robert Bernasconi and Simon Critchley, 234–45. London: Athlone, 1991.

Lopez, Barry. *Of Wolves and Men.* New York: Scribner's, 1978.

Margulis, Lynn, and Dorion Sagan. *What Is Life?* Berkeley and Los Angeles: University of California Press, 2000.

Martin, Bernard. *Great Twentieth Century Jewish Philosophers: Shestov, Rosenzweig, Buber, with Selections from Their Writings.* New York: Macmillan, 1969.

———. "Introduction: The Life and Thought of Lev Shestov." In *Athens and Jerusalem,* 11–44. New York: Simon and Schuster, 1968.

Mathews, Freya. "Ceres: Singing up the City." *PAN: Philosophy, Activism, Nature* 1 (2000): 5–15.

———. *For Love of Matter: A Contemporary Panpsychism.* Albany: State University of New York Press, 2003.

Mellor, Mary. *Feminism and Ecology.* Cambridge: Polity Press, 1997.

Milton, Kay. "Fear for the Future." *Australian Journal of Anthropology* 19, no. 1 (2008): 73–76.

Mitchell, Stephen. *Into the Whirlwind: A Translation of the Book of Job.* Garden City: Doubleday, 1979.

Morey, Darcy. "Burying Key Evidence: The Social Bond between Dogs and People." *Journal of Archaeological Science* 33 (2006): 158–75.

Newton, Adam. *Narrative Ethics.* Cambridge: Harvard University Press, 1995.

O'Neill, Adam. *Living with the Dingo.* Sydney: Envirobooks, 2002.

Oppenheim, Michael. *Speaking/Writing of God: Jewish Reflections on the Life with Others.* Albany: State University of New York Press, 1997.

Parfit, Derek. "The Puzzle of Reality: Why Does the Universe Exist?" In *Metaphysics: The Big Questions,* edited by Peter van Inwagen and Dean Zimmerman, 418–27. Malden: Blackwell, 1998.

Phipps, William. "The Plight of the Song of Songs." In *The Song of Songs,* edited by Harold Bloom, 5–32. New York: Chelsea House, 1988.

Pickard, John. "Predator-Proof Fences for Biodiversity Conservation: Some Lessons from Dingo Fences." In *Animals of Arid Australia: Out on Their Own?* edited by Chris Dickman, Daniel Lunney, and Shelley Burgin, 197–207. Mosman: Royal Zoological Society of New South Wales, 2007.

Plaskow, Judith. *Standing Again at Sinai: Judaism from a Feminist Perspective.* San Francisco: Harper and Row, 1990.

Plato. *Phaedrus.* Translated by R. Hackforth. Cambridge: Cambridge University Press, 1997.

Plumwood, Val. "Being Prey." http://valplumwood.com/2008/03/08/being-prey/.

——. *Feminism and the Mastery of Nature.* London: Routledge, 1993.

——. "Tasteless: Towards a Food-Based Approach to Death." *Environmental Values* 17, no. 3 (2008): 323–31.

Pope, Marvin. "Interpretations of the Sublime Song: Love and Death." In *The Song of Songs,* edited by Harold Bloom, 25–48. New York: Chelsea House, 1998.

Prigogine, Ilya. *The End of Certainty: Time, Chaos and the New Laws of Nature.* New York: Free Press, 1997.

Quammen, David. *The Song of the Dodo: Island Biogeography in an Age of Extinctions.* New York: Scribner, 1996.

Rigby, Kate. *Topographies of the Sacred: The Poetics of Place in European Romanticism.* Charlottesville: University of Virginia Press, 2004.

Robinson, Roland. *Altjeringa and Other Aboriginal Poems.* Sydney: A. H. and A. W. Reed, 1970.

Rose, Deborah Bird. *Dingo Makes Us Human.* Cambridge: Cambridge University Press, 2000.

——. *Hidden Histories: Black Stories from Victoria River Downs, Humbert River, and Wave Hill Stations, North Australia.* Canberra: Aboriginal Studies Press, 1991.

———. "'Moral Friends' in the Zone of Disaster." *Tamkang Review* 37, no. 1 (Autumn 2006): 7–97.

———. *Reports from a Wild Country: Ethics for Decolonisation.* Sydney: University of New South Wales Press, 2004.

Rubenstein, Richard L. *After Auschwitz: History, Theology, and Contemporary Judaism.* Baltimore: Johns Hopkins Univ. Press, 1992.

"Safe Use of 1080 Poison." www.agric.wa.gov.au/agency/pubns/farmnote/1996/T10596.html.

Scarry, Elaine. *The Body in Pain: The Making and Unmaking of the World.* New York: Oxford University Press, 1985.

Schreiner, Susan. *Where Shall Wisdom Be Found?: Calvin's Exegesis of Job from Medieval and Modern Perspectives.* Chicago: University of Chicago Press, 1994.

Schwartz, Regina. *The Curse of Cain: The Violent Legacy of Monotheism.* Chicago: University of Chicago Press, 1997.

Sebald, W. G. "Campo Santo." *Words without Borders: The Online Magazine for International Literature.* 2005. http://wordswithoutborders.org/article/campo-santo/.

Shepard, Paul. *The Others: How Animals Made Us Human.* Washington, D.C.: Island Press, 1996.

Shestov, Lev. *Athens and Jerusalem.* Translated by Bernard Martin. New York: Simon and Schuster, 1968.

———. "Myth and Truth: On the Metaphysics of Knowledge." In *Speculation and Revelation,* by Shestov, 118–29. Athens: Ohio University Press, 1982a.

———. "Speculation and Apocalypse: The Religious Philosophy of Vladimir Solovyov." In *Speculation and Revelation,* by Shestov, 18–88. Athens: Ohio University Press, 1982c.

———. *Speculation and Revelation.* New York: Simon and Schuster, 1982b.

Soloveitchik, Joseph. *The Lonely Man of Faith.* New York: Three Leaves Press; Doubleday, 2006.

Steeves, Peter. "Lost Dog." In *The Things Themselves: Phenomenology and the Return to the Everyday,* 49–63. Albany: State University of New York Press, 2006.

Tanakh: The Holy Scriptures. The New JPS Translation According to the Traditional Hebrew Text. Philadelphia: Jewish Publication Society, 1985.

Taylor, Tamara. "The Origins of the Mastiff." *Canis Max* (Winter 1996–97). http://people.unt.edu/~tlt0002/mastiff.htm

"1080 Poison." www.geocities.com/littlenails/Bib1080Poison.html.

Thubron, Colin. *The Lost Heart of Asia.* New York: HarperCollins, 1994.

"Transcript of Proceedings: North West Simpson Desert Land Claim (No. 126)." Adelaide: Commonwealth Reporting Service, Commonwealth of Australia, 1990.

Tsing, Anna. "Unruly Edges: Mushrooms as Companion Species." In *NatureCultures: Thinking with Donna Haraway,* edited by S. Ghamari-Tabrizi. Cambridge: MIT Press, forthcoming.

Tumarkin, Maria. *Traumascapes: The Power and Fate of Places Transformed by Tragedy*. Melbourne: Melbourne University Press, 2005.

Twain, Mark. [Samuel Clemens]. "Following the Equator: A Journey around the World." *Harper's*, 1903. In *Following the Equator.* www.classicbookshelf.com/library/mark_twain/following_the_eqator.

———. *The Adventures of Tom Sawyer and the Adventures of Huckleberry Finn.* 1936. New York: Heritage Press, 1940.

van Dooren, Thom. "Being-with-Death: Heidegger, Levinas, Derrida & Bataille on Death." Honor's thesis, 2002.

Wallach, Arian, and Adam O'Neill. *Persistence of Endangered Species: Is the Dingo the Key?* Report for DEH Wildlife Conservation Fund, 2008.

Whaley, Joachim. Introduction to *Mirrors of Mortality: Studies in the Social History of Death,* edited by Whaley, 1–14. London: Europa, 1981.

Wiesel, Ellie. "Job: Our Contemporary." In *Messengers of God: Biblical Portraits and Legends,* 211–35. New York: Random House, 1985.

———. "A Plea for the Dead." In *Legends of Our Time,* by Wiesel, 213–37. New York: Avon Books, 1970.

Wilson, Edward O. *The Future of Life*. New York: Knopf, 2002.

Wolfe, Cary. *Animal Rites: American Culture, the Discourse of Species, and Post-humanist Theory*. Chicago: University of Chicago Press, 2003.

Woodford, James. *The Dog Fence: A Journey across the Heart of Australia*. Melbourne: Text, 2003.

Wright, Tamra. "Beyond the 'Eclipse of God': The *Shoah* in the Jewish Thought of Buber and Levinas." In *Levinas & Buber: Dialogue & Difference,* edited by Peter Atterton, Matthew Calarco, and Maurice Friedman, 203–55. Pittsburgh: Duquesne University Press, 2004.

Wyschogrod, Edith. *Emmanuel Levinas: The Problem of Ethical Metaphysics*. New York: Fordham University Press, 2000.

———. *Spirit in Ashes: Hegel, Heidegger, and Man-Made Mass Death*. New Haven: Yale University Press, 1985.

Index

Page numbers in boldface refer to definitions; page numbers in italics refer to illustrations.

Rachel Stein
Shifting the Ground: American Women Writers' Revisions of Nature, Gender, and Race

Ian Marshall
Story Line: Exploring the Literature of the Appalachian Trail

Patrick D. Murphy
Farther Afield in the Study of Nature-Oriented Literature

Bernard W. Quetchenbach
Back from the Far Field: American Nature Poetry in the Late Twentieth Century

Karla Armbruster and Kathleen R. Wallace, editors
Beyond Nature Writing: Expanding the Boundaries of Ecocriticism

Stephen Adams
The Best and Worst Country in the World: Perspectives on the Early Virginia Landscape

Mark Allister
Refiguring the Map of Sorrow: Nature Writing and Autobiography

Ralph H. Lutts
The Nature Fakers: Wildlife, Science, and Sentiment (reprint)

Michael A. Bryson
Visions of the Land: Science, Literature, and the American Environment from the Era of Exploration to the Age of Ecology

Robert Bernard Hass
Going by Contraries: Robert Frost's Conflict with Science

Ian Marshall
Peak Experiences: Walking Meditations on Literature, Nature, and Need

Glen A. Love
Practical Ecocriticism: Literature, Biology, and the Environment

Scott Herring
Lines on the Land: Writers, Art, and the National Parks

Heike Schaefer
Gender, Genre, and Geography: Mary Austin's Concept and Practice of Regionalism

Mark Allister, editor
Eco-Man: New Perspectives on Masculinity and Nature

Kate Rigby
Topographies of the Sacred: The Poetics of Place in European Romanticism

Alan Williamson
Westernness: A Meditation

John Elder
Pilgrimage to Vallombrosa: From Vermont to Italy in the Footsteps of George Perkins Marsh

Mary Ellen Bellanca
Daybooks of Discovery: Nature Diaries in Britain, 1770–1870

Rinda West
Out of the Shadow: Ecopsychology, Story, and Encounters with the Land

Bonnie Roos and Alex Hunt, editors
Postcolonial Green: Environmental Politics and World Narratives

Paula Willoquet-Maricondi, editor
Framing the World: Explorations in Ecocriticism and Film

Deborah Bird Rose
Wild Dog Dreaming: Love and Extinction